David Worshiped With a Fervent Faith

David Worshiped With a Fervent Faith

by
Judson Cornwall, Th.D.

Destiny Image Publishers
P.O. Box 310
Shippensburg, PA 17257

"Speaking to the Purposes of God for This Generation"

Library of Congress Catalog Card Number: 92-074509
ISBN: 1-56043-089-3

For Worldwide Distribution
Printed in the U.S.A.

First printing: 1993
Second printing: 1994

Destiny Image books are available through these fine distributors outside the United States:

Christian Growth, Inc.
Jalan Kilang-Timor, Singapore 0315

Successful Christian Living
Capetown, Rep. of South Africa

Lifestream
Nottingham, England

Vision Resources
Ponsonby, Auckland, New Zealand

Rhema Ministries Trading
Randburg, South Africa

WA Buchanan Company
Geebung, Queensland, Australia

Salvation Book Centre
Petaling, Jaya, Malaysia

Word Alive
Niverville, Manitoba, Canada

Inside the U.S., call toll free to order:
1-800-722-6774

Dedication

To *Ressa Slaybaugh*, a family friend since college days. Her faith has remained unshaken.

Contents

Preface

Faith may be a New Testament word, but it was gloriously experienced in Old Testament times. All the heroes and heroines of faith listed in the eleventh chapter of the Book of Hebrews were Old Testament characters whose walk with God inspired an active, living faith. David is one of those persons.

David lacked the advantage of our New Testament, and there is no indication that he understood the advent of Jesus, but he came to know God in such an intimate way that faith flowed into and out of his heart like an eternal river.

When David heard from God, whether it was through a prophet, by the priest's use of the Urim and Thummim, or by inner inspiration, he acted upon what he was told. This is faith at its highest level. Faith cannot remain an attitude. It produces action. In the Hebrews list of faith's heroes and heroines, the words "by faith ..." are always followed by a description of the action of the person to whom faith was imparted.

The more I studied the life of David, the more I was convinced of the vast magnitude of faith. It starts in God, works through people and effects the will of God in our natural world. It does not flow through persons as neutral channels, but consistently affects their lives. Faith will alter and enlarge the person who lets it flow, changing his or her attitudes and giving a passion for God he or she did not possess before faith's presence was made known.

David did not create his faith. He received it from God, revitalized his life with it and then released it toward whatever pressing problem he was experiencing. David does not seem to have moved in and out of his faith very often. He maintained his faith, lived in his faith, and worshiped in his faith. This is why we are so inspired in our personal worship when we join David by reading one of his psalms. David joyed in his faith through song, and when we sing along with him, we enter into that same joy.

Many of the principles shared in this book were shared much earlier in my book *Unfeigned Faith*, which has been out of print for many years. These truths seemed too vital for today's Christians to leave them unpublished. They are so rewritten, rearranged and edited that only the most avid student of my writings will recognize them. I have so few such readers that I am not worried about criticism for repetition.

Judson Cornwall
Phoenix, Arizona

Chapter 1

David Received His Faith

Faith's Source

High on the western slopes of the Rocky Mountains in British Columbia, Canada, three men stood motionless. The only sound that broke the silence was the gentle bubbling of a small spring gushing forth fresh mountain water from beneath an enormous rock that appeared to hang precariously on the mountainside. The evergreens that surrounded them formed a lush background for the rich reds and yellows of the deciduous trees that found sufficient soil in this rocky environment. As He does each fall in this part of the world, the Divine Artist had painted lavishly with special colors.

The men stood silently, staring at the panoramic view of progressively colored vegetation. It seemed to them that God had dropped His rainbow to the earth as nature prepared for the cold blast of winter by sending many of her trees and shrubs into a dormant state. They wondered if they would be the only people to see this year's painting.

Weary from an unproductive day of hunting for elk, the men dropped their backpacks onto the ground and carefully set their rifles on top of them. Then they dropped to their knees and stooped to bury their faces in the flowing stream, drinking deeply of the cool, refreshing water.

Having slacked their thirst and refilled their canteens, the hunters leaned against the protruding rock, making themselves comfortable on the small shelf of level ground that the flow of water had carved in the mountain. "You might be interested to know," the guide said, "that this is the source of the mighty Columbia River. It is the fourth largest river on the North American continent. It begins here in Canada, runs south into Washington and then flows from east to west, forming the border between the states of Washington and Oregon."

Geographically speaking, the guide was correct. That mountain spring is the beginning of the Columbia River; but it is not the river's actual source. One must go to the ocean to find its source, for it is the ocean waters evaporated by the heat of the sun and carried as clouds by winds to the mountain peaks that cause the deep winter snows that feed this spring.

The guide's assumption is a common misconception. We often mistake the source of the channel for the source of the flow. We speak of Abraham's faith as though he were the originator of it, but the Bible prefers to say: "By faith Abraham ... went out, not knowing where he was going" (Hebrews 11:8). The biblical writer further develops this theme when he assures us one chapter later that *Jesus* is "the author and finisher of our faith" (Hebrews 12:2). Faith begins and ends in God.

Therefore, the faith that first surfaced in David, giving him a divine unction for worship, had its source in Almighty God. David was never the author or originator of that faith. He merely received and released it.

God anticipated what David would become

There is something wonderfully consistent about the divine viewpoint. God, who sits in eternity, views everything from an "eternal now" perspective. He sees the end from the beginning and proclaims as reality that which has not yet come into existence. Since He has the power to accomplish His eternal purposes, He considers as complete whatever He commences.

The only variables in this process are the tools that God uses to fulfill His purposes. No matter how divinely chosen, marvelously equipped, or spiritually anointed an individual may be, no person is indispensable to the work of the Lord. Israel's first king is a prime example of this truth.

Everything about the choice of Saul for rulership in Israel had a touch of the divine. God selected him twice — once privately and once publicly. Jehovah gave him unusual spiritual experiences and even changed his heart. God also gave Saul a unique capacity as a military leader and prompted helpers to gather around him. Still, as sometimes happens, when Saul became strong in his reign, his heart turned from obeying God to relying on the convenient and the expedient. He exchanged faith for function and lost all the benefits that his faith had provided. "So Samuel said to him, 'The LORD has torn the kingdom of Israel from you today, and has given it to a neighbor of yours, who is better than you' " (1 Samuel 15:28).

This encounter was painful for Samuel, who mourned over Saul for a long season. "Then the LORD said to Samuel, 'How long will you mourn for Saul, seeing I have rejected him from reigning over Israel? Fill your horn with oil, and go; I am sending you to Jesse the Bethlehemite. For I have provided Myself a king among his sons' " (1 Samuel 16:1). Under the guise of offering a family sacrifice at Bethlehem,

Samuel moved fearfully to obey the Lord's command. One by one Jesse's sons stood before Samuel, each expecting to be anointed king of Israel. But God refused even the prophet's assessment of these men.

Thus Jesse made seven of his sons pass before Samuel. And Samuel said to Jesse, "The LORD has not chosen these." And Samuel said to Jesse, "Are all the young men here?" Then he said, "There remains yet the youngest, and there he is, keeping the sheep." And Samuel said to Jesse, "Send and bring him. For we will not sit down till he comes here" (1 Samuel 16:10-11).

We can only imagine the anger and the frustration that David's older brothers felt when Samuel delayed the sacrifice and the fellowship meal to wait for their despised brother to come from the sheep, to get cleaned up and to be presented to the prophet. How much stronger their anger and frustration must have become when David finally arrived, for the Scriptures say: "So he sent and brought him in. Now he was ruddy, with bright eyes, and good-looking. And the LORD said, 'Arise, anoint him; for this is the one!' " (1 Samuel 16:12)

How could Jehovah so honor the one they had chosen to dishonor? Is it possible that David and God had developed a personal relationship while David dealt with his loneliness in the long evening hours by playing and singing songs onto Jehovah? Perhaps it is this private acquaintance with Him that causes God to esteem those who are so disdained by the religious people of our generation.

God chose David

The psalmist Asaph wrote, "He also chose David His servant, and took him from the sheepfolds; from following the ewes that had young He brought him, to shepherd Jacob His people, and Israel His inheritance" (Psalm 78:70-71). God had already determined that David would be chosen as the second king of Israel before He insisted that Samuel call for Jesse's youngest son to leave the sheep in the field and come to the sacrifice. Jehovah made this choice. It was not a family decision; nor were the residents of Bethlehem given a vote. This was not a democratic action; it was theocratic. Samuel did not interview David or inform him of the situation. He did not even allow David to express an opinion. God simply said to David, "I choose you!" All David needed was sufficient faith to accept what God had said.

Although modern evangelism frequently puts a heavy emphasis upon choosing God, the Bible consistently emphasizes that God has chosen us. The Old Testament widely illustrates this. The New Testament loudly proclaims it. Jesus told His disciples, "You did not choose Me, but I chose you and appointed you ..." (John 15:16) Paul places God's choice in precreation days, for he wrote: " ... He chose us in Him before the foundation of the world, that we should be holy and without blame before Him in love" (Ephesians 1:4); " ... God from the beginning chose you for salvation through sanctification by the Spirit and belief in the truth" (2 Thessalonians 2:13).

Just as David's only option was to receive or reject God's choice, so we are required to simply accept God's choices and flow with them in faith. We do not need to seek to be chosen by God. Our worthiness does not enter the decision. Because God decided our future before forming the world, and we did not exist then, neither our good points nor our bad points influenced His decision.

As God sent Samuel to David, so He sends His Spirit to inform us of His choice. "The Spirit Himself bears witness with our spirit that we are children of God ..." (Romans 8:16) "And because you are sons,

God has sent forth the Spirit of His Son into your hearts, crying out, 'Abba, Father!' " (Galatians 4:6) This Spirit is the "spirit of faith."

In one quick anointing, David was called from the life of a shepherd to the responsibilities of a king. This change, of course, was provisional. David would experience a lengthy season of preparation for his new position. His transformation from a shepherd to a king was progressive. As Bob Mumford loves to say, "Between God's calling and His commissioning lies God's college." God offered David no shortcuts. Neither does this God, "who changes not," provide quick fixes for us. God's choice becomes our challenge to change. Although we do nothing to motivate God to *choose* us, there is much we must do to enable God to *use* us. He bases His choices on what faith can enable us to become, not on what we are when He calls us.

After David's long and faithful reign, he is described as "the man raised up on high, the anointed of the God of Jacob, and the sweet psalmist of Israel" (2 Samuel 23:1). When Samuel summoned David from the field, he was none of these. God, however, saw what He could produce in this young man. He foresaw the end from the beginning, and it pleased Him.

God raised up David

The statement, "the man raised up on high," is powerful, for the Hebrew word used for "high" is *al*, which means the Highest (i.e. God). David was raised to Jehovah. Far more than lifting Jesse's youngest son from farm boy to king, God raised David to Himself. David sought personal communion with Jehovah. He learned how to come into the divine presence. The blessing of knowing and serving God is evident in the many times God lifted this fugitive trainee from the pits of discouragement to the heights of celestial worship by an impartation of divine faith.

While we can easily recognize David's delight in God during his songfests in the cool of the evening, these occasions were not David's primary times of worship. God taught David to worship in the everyday activities of life. Through David, God taught His people for generations to come that worship is more than a song or a sacrifice. Worship is a lifestyle. By faith, David worshiped in warfare as he subdued Israel's enemies and brought peace to the land. His attitudes and actions in government reveal his faithful worship as he ruled with integrity and justice. David also worshiped God faithfully in his family relationships and his daily friendships.

David's life exemplifies the life of a true worshiper. Many generations after David, Paul taught: "Therefore, whether you eat or drink, or whatever you do, do all to the glory of God" (1 Corinthians 10:31). This perspective in no way detracts from the importance and the beauty of David's worship in song, dance and the use of instruments that I presented in my previous two books on David's worship (*David Worshiped a Living God* and *Worship as David Lived It*). Rather, it balances David's recognized greatness in these areas of worship by acknowledging that David's worship did not cease when he left the tabernacle or dismissed the choir. Worship was not a segment of David's life; it was the totality of his life. Divine faith lifted David up to Jehovah in his day-to-day activities.

Since worship is far more than performance, worship that is acceptable and pleasing in God's sight requires the faith to adjust the lifestyle of the worshiper. A song or a sacrifice does not impress God nearly as much as the singer or the one making the sacrifice. It is people, not presentations, that release worship. True acts of worship are merely the methods and the forms the worshiper uses to express the love and adoration toward God that flows from a life of faith, for "... without faith it is impossible to please Him, for he who comes to God must believe that He is, and that He is a rewarder of those who diligently seek Him" (Hebrews 11:6).

When God chose David and raised him to Himself, He imparted a great measure of faith into David's life. That faith was far more than the faith that is as natural to man as the air he breathes. Witness a newborn baby's absolute trust and faith in its mother, or the faith people evidence in machinery, public services and government. Without this human faith, society would become a perpetual struggle for assurance. God has mercifully implanted inherent trust and faith in every human heart. It is part of the life process.

Fortunately, God has a divine faith that is higher, different and far more glorious than human faith. While each faith is a gift or provision of God that functions in our realm of space and time, only divine faith can function in eternity. Likewise, everyone has natural faith, but only those who come to God through Jesus Christ can become partakers of God's supernatural faith. David was such a participant.

God anointed David

David was "the anointed of the God of Jacob" (2 Samuel 23:1). This anointing began in Bethlehem at the family sacrifice. We read: "Then Samuel took the horn of oil and anointed him in the midst of his brothers; and the Spirit of the LORD came upon David from that day forward" (1 Samuel 16:13). In that brief moment, a simple, outward ceremony united David with God in an intimate, personal way. Faith, which in the absolute sense of the word is a personal and spiritual union with God, entered David's life. This kingly anointing brought such an indwelling of the Spirit of the LORD to David that God dwelt in this chosen man and lived through him.

Faith always requires more than a difficulty, a demanding need or a dependable promise. Faith flows out of a living, loving correlation between the saint and the Savior. This union of God with the individual believer becomes the absolute of faith. Faith cannot exist apart from God, because it is a foundational part of God Himself. Jesus urged us to "have the faith of God" (Mark 11:22, marginal reading). The more vital our union with God is, the more vital will be His faith within us. To share God's nature, we must share His presence. This is why He has sent His Spirit to dwell within us. David later discovered that the indwelling Spirit exercised all the faith he ever needed.

In his devotional book *My Utmost for His Highest*, Oswald Chambers wrote: "Faith is the whole man rightly related to God by the power of the Spirit of Jesus Christ." Both Saul and David received this divine anointing. The difference between the two is that David learned to live righteously before God and His Word, while Saul did not.

God is the source of our faith, and the presence of the Spirit of God is the channel through which faith flows into our lives. God's primary purpose for placing the Spirit of faith in our lives is not so much to *empower us do*, as to *enable us to become*. As the apostle testified, " ... as He is, so are we in this world" (1 John 4:17). Merely saying what Christ said, or even believing what He believed, does not produce faith. We must become what He was. Central to that transformation is our need to share His intimate fellowship with the Father and to be partakers of His divine nature. Only then will we experience the forceful flow of genuine faith that permeated Christ's life.

The faith we see in David's daily worship had its beginning in his divine anointing. This anointing was a singular experience for Saul and a continuous experience for David. So precious was God's Spirit to this king of Israel that he cried to the Lord as he wallowed in his sin of adultery, "Do not cast me away from Your presence, and do not take Your Holy Spirit from me" (Psalm 51:11).

David's lifetime of worship was centered in his desire to live in communion with the Spirit of God. He had witnessed the consequences when God removed His Spirit from Saul. The devastation that entered Saul's life provided a strong impetus for David to continually seek the Lord's presence. He didn't want a demonic spirit to replace the Spirit of the Lord in his life.

God eulogized David's sweetness

David's position as the singing psalmist of Israel is the theme of the next chapter. The closing summary in Second Samuel describes him as "the sweet psalmist of Israel" (2 Samuel 23:1). There is something important in this description of David that goes beyond his worship through music. The emphasis here is on the word "sweet." The Hebrew word used to describe David is *na'iym*, which means "delightful or pleasant." So special is this word that the Holy Spirit used it only twice in the Bible. It comes from the root *na'em*, which means "to be agreeable, to be a delight, to be pleasant, to be sweet."

In addition to *na'iym*, there are five or six other Hebrew words used in the Scriptures that are translated "sweet." From these words, we can begin to understand what is sweet to God. Everything that God calls "sweet" is connected with worship. We read in Exodus that sweet spices were mixed in the anointing oil (Exodus 30:23,34). The incense burned on the Golden Altar in the Tabernacle in the Wilderness was described as "sweet incense" by God (Exodus 25:6). He also called the sacrifices offered on the Brazen Altar a "sweet aroma" (Exodus 29:18).

Since we inexorably associate David with worship, it is fitting that God would speak of David as "sweet." There was a fragrance in the life of David that pleased the nostrils of God, and it all began when the prophet poured the anointing oil on David's head. God shared the sweetness of the Holy Spirit with this chosen man, and David never lost that fragrance.

The fragrance of God's Spirit was also given to others. The kings who followed David were anointed with oil, as was King Saul, who preceded him. Yet, King Saul—whose choice and anointing involved more divine involvement and intervention than the selection of any other king over Israel—is known as the willful king, and King Solomon—whose anointing David himself supervised—is known as the wise king. Only David is described by God as "sweet."

This title does not suggest that David was effeminate or extremely gentle in his nature. He was a skilled outdoorsman and a ferocious fighter. He successfully molded rebels into a fighting unit that no nation could withstand. No, David was not weak. He possessed great strength of character and was renowned for his skills in leadership and statesmanship. His enemies did not see his sweetness, for they experienced his wrath. Only God saw David as sweet, because David's worship ascended to Him as a sweet aroma of praise and adoration.

One of the surprises of heaven will be to discover how differently God viewed certain people. Some whom we have considered great will be unveiled as frauds. Some who have been unknowns on earth will be celebrities in heaven. Some who were judged as stern disciplinarians will be revealed as sweet in the sight of God. It is ever true that "... the Lord does not see as man sees; for man looks at the outward appearance, but the LORD looks at the heart" (1 Samuel 16:7).

God's faith made David sweet

David was neither the first nor the last king to worship Jehovah. Although other kings and leaders offered sacrifices and sang songs to Jehovah, it is David alone that God calls "sweet." It must be that David received faith from God and learned to release a high level of faith in his worship of Jehovah. Faith is the key to our entire relationship with God. We are "saved through faith" (Ephesians 2:8), "sanctified by faith" (Acts 26:18), "justified by faith" (Galatians 2:16), and "kept ... through faith" (1 Peter 1:5).

We all enter the graces of God through the doorway of faith, for Paul wrote,

> *Therefore, having been justified by faith, we have peace with God through our Lord Jesus Christ, through whom also **we have access by faith** into this grace in which we stand, and rejoice in hope of the glory of God* (Romans 5:1-2).

God, and the word He speaks to men and women, is the source of true faith. The Bible plainly declares this, and the life of Christ illustrates it: When Jesus spoke to needy ones, they acted immediately. The many heroes and heroines of faith listed in the eleventh chapter of Hebrews responded to a word from God in nearly unbelievable actions. David was a good listener. He responded in faith to the word and the presence of God in his life. This was the sweetness to which God refers.

If faith is to be produced in our hearts, we must hear the word of God as a beneficiary listens to the reading of a will or an accused gives his attention to the sentence of a judge. What we hear will affect us for eternity, for it is the infinite God who speaks. His words impart a small measure of the atmosphere of eternity into our limited sphere of daily life. Careless listening will produce human frailty, because divine faith is not formed in the emotions of men's minds. The faith that flows from God is produced in the divine nature and released to us through His inspired Word. Therefore, we always have an abundance of faith available to us. The confession that we lack faith is thus often a confession that we have spent insufficient time in God's presence and in His Word.

David's worship always brought him into God's presence, where he both heard God's voice and responded to His directives. This is the ingredient that made David's worship sweet to God — the sweet ingredient of faith.

The provision of this sweet component of faith is entirely up to God. He alone is the source of faith. Yet we need not fear that faith will become unavailable to us, for God never fails to keep the covenants He makes with men and women. God does not demand faith from us and then leave it up to us to produce it. He merely asks us to hear with our hearts and speak with our mouths that which He has already spoken into existence. Thus, we do not create faith by our words; we simply speak the faith that already exists. When we receive this faith by speaking what we hear God saying, marvelous things happen. If, however, we are exposed to faith through the hearing of the Word, and we do not respond, nothing is produced and our worship lacks the sweet fragrance so desired by God.

David, anointed of God to become Israel's king, did not immediately ascend to that office. Yet, without delay, he became a sweet worshiper of Jehovah. Whether a shepherd on the hillside or the court musician of a rejected king, David sang praises to God. He did not need position to offer God the sweet incense of praise and worship. Neither do we. David's lifestyle of daily worship is an example that bids us to offer to the Lord the sweet worship He desires.

Chapter 2

David Joyed in His Faith

Faith's Song

Lying on their backs while staring aimlessly at the changing shapes of the clouds in the turquoise-blue sky, the men began to tune into the sound of the flowing water. "The spring is singing a happy song!" one of the men said.

"If it knew all it will endure before it gets to the ocean, this brook wouldn't be so happy," the melancholic member of this trio of hunters replied. "The lake at the base of this mountain will so swallow this stream that it will lose its identity. Falls will dash it on rocks and churn it to foam. Dams will restrict it, and human waste will pollute it. Boats of all sizes will invade its water, and loaded barges will use it as a highway. Farmers will steal much of it for irrigation, and the sun will evaporate great portions of it. The small portion that survives will constantly flow downward. That's not much to sing about."

Undaunted by the pessimism of his companion, the first man replied, "Maybe this singing stream knows it will return as snow — according to the Creator's plan — and complete the cycle in unending rotation. Maybe this is not a song of ignorance, but of faith. Perhaps the stream trusts the Creator's plan."

Faith sings a song of trust

Although Saul was Israel's first king, David was well aware of the histories of the surrounding nations. Their absolute monarchies had proven that it is dangerous to be proclaimed king while the reigning monarch still lives. He was also mindful of the Old Testament stories that told of the slaughter of all contenders to the throne. He knew that Samuel's anointing put his life in jeopardy. Yet fear was not evident in David's life as he nonchalantly returned to his duties as a shepherd.

"Commit your way to the Lord, trust also in Him, and He shall bring it to pass"... "O my God, I trust in You; let me not be ashamed; let not my enemies triumph over me" (Psalm 37:5; 25:2). David's confidence was in the Lord, not in himself. He was convinced that if God called him, He could also place him on the throne.

As a scheduled airliner tossed like a child's kite in the storm high above the Pacific Ocean, the passengers regressed from alarm to fear, and even the stewardesses reached for airsickness bags. Some passengers cursed to release their tension. Others cried. A few prayed. Everyone seemed gripped by terror — everyone, that is, except one woman who was traveling in the first-class section of the plane.

"Why aren't you afraid?" one passenger shouted at her.

Calmly turning her head toward the inquirer, while momentarily setting her needlepoint on her lap, she quietly said, "My husband is the pilot on this flight, and he is well qualified to get us to the airport safely."

The existence of this story testifies to the fact that the plane and its passengers did, in fact, arrive safely at the airport. By the time they landed, however, it is very likely that most of the passengers had become distraught, emotionally spent and physically ill. Only one passenger remained calm and collected. Why? She had put her faith in someone!

David may have instinctively known, or he may have been taught by the Spirit of God, that the object of faith and trust must be God. Faith in self is reckless, faith in faith is ridiculous, and faith in others is risky. This Old Testament king knew that the object of his faith was far more valuable than the faith itself. He had found God to be reliable. He wrote: "The testimony of the Lord is sure, making wise the simple" (Psalm 19:7). God never needs to take an oath before giving testimony, for He is the truth (John 14:6) and He cannot lie (Numbers 23:19).

During the subjugation of the nations that surrounded Israel, David's brilliant military strategy was little more than following divine orders. God's word to Him proved to be astute. David's faith in what God said enabled him to give reliable leadership to both his armies and the entire nation of Israel. He had learned to make faith practical. Since God believed everything He said, David chose to join God in this belief and to acted obediently on God's instructions.

Why should we wonder, then, that David wrote: "Blessed are all those who put their trust in Him" (Psalm 2:12). "Let all those rejoice who put their trust in You; let them ever shout for joy, because You defend them; let those also who love Your name be joyful in You" (Psalm 5:11). Even when the threat of death was hanging over his head, David could still sing a song of trust.

Faith's song gets attention

God transferred to David the kingly anointing that had rested upon Saul. We read: "But the Spirit of the LORD departed from Saul, and a distressing spirit from the LORD troubled him" (1 Samuel 16:14). Although God allowed Saul to live and to continue in his rebellious ways, Saul's life was not enjoyable. So harassed was Israel's first king by the demonic spirit that God commissioned to torment him, that temper tantrums and violent acts threatened the lives of those around him. Out of either a need for self-preservation, or maybe just a genuine concern for their master, the household servants asked Saul, "Let our master now command your servants, who are before you, to seek out a man who is a skillful player on the harp; and it shall be that he will play it with his hand when the distressing spirit from God is upon you, and you shall be well" (1 Samuel 16:16). We do not know what prompted Saul's servants to make this request, for this is the first time in the Bible that music was used to control demonic activity.

Saul quickly granted permission for the search, and the servants chose David. It seems that David was well known to some of these servants of Saul, for we read: "Then one of the servants answered and said, 'Look, I have seen a son of Jesse the Bethlehemite, who is skillful in playing, a mighty man of valor, a man of war, prudent in speech, and a handsome person; and the LORD is with him' " (1 Samuel 16:18).

Just as the brook sings silently in the mountains, completely unaware that its music will ever be heard, so David released his faith and trust in Jehovah without the slightest awareness that he was being observed by a servant of King Saul. His song was much more than the simple ballad that came from his lips, for faith sang its own song of courage through David.

Thus, the servant reported far more than David's musical ability. Captivated by the man as well as the music, the servant said of him: "[He is] a mighty man of valor, a man of war, [and] prudent in speech." All this the servant learned by listening to David sing. Until this description of David given by Saul's servant, we have no record of David's involvement in natural warfare. But when faith sings, it releases in words what it will later release in works.

This reporter added that David was a handsome person, and that the LORD was with him. God's inner presence so affected David's outer countenance that the servant knew the Lord was with him. In keeping with the words Moses had written much earlier — "And let the beauty of the LORD our God be upon us" (Psalm 90:17) — David's faith affected his face.

Some people speak of faith as an attitude that incites an action. When that action is a song, there are no secrets left because the Spirit of faith loves to sing of God's mighty power and His magnificent promises. David was no exception to this rule. He was so convinced that embraced faith and trust in Jehovah was the strength of his life that he declared in one of his songs: "My soul shall make its boast in the LORD; the humble shall hear of it and be glad" (Psalm 34:2).

David also knew that faith's song can strengthen the lives of others. Thus, he yielded himself and the gift God had given him to worship through music to be a constant source of encouragement to his associates: "He has put a new song in my mouth — praise to our God; many will see it and fear, and will trust in the LORD" (Psalm 40:3).

Faith's song brings us before kings

It is one thing to have an anointing to serve; it is an entirely different matter to know how to serve. David's role as protector of his father's sheep isolated him from life in Saul's court. Perhaps he wondered how he would learn to be a king, for he certainly could not learn court protocol on the hillside with the sheep. Neither dared he seek help from others, for that would have invited disaster. No, he could not parade his calling or in any way reveal that he had been anointed by Samuel to be king.

David seemed to realize that ministry will make room for itself. He knew that if God had called him, He would have to qualify him and place him. Therefore, instead of seeking advancement, David continued to sing. It was his singing that eventually brought him into the king's palace.

David was summoned for a command performance. In response to the report of his servant, "... Saul sent messengers to Jesse, and said, 'Send me your son David, who is with the sheep' " (1 Samuel 16:19). If Saul's demand produced nervousness in David, it did not show. Having sung before the King of kings and the LORD of lords, why would Saul seem like such an awesome audience? David simply relied on a much-used theme, "Shout joyfully to the LORD, all the earth; break forth in song, rejoice, and sing praises" (Psalm 98:4).

Although David's musical recital on the harp became his first step to the throne, we must be careful to recognize that far more than practiced skill brought David to Saul's court. God had anointed David with a kingly anointing. For the moment this anointing was released musically — for higher anointings can always flow in lower channels. When this happens, excellence is the result.

Through this experience, David learned what modern Christians need to learn. A divine anointing does not need an office to be effective. It just needs a yielded vessel through which to flow. David was a willing vessel. Although the prophet had declared that his anointing was for kingship, David allowed God's Spirit to sing through him. Logic would say that David should have confronted Saul; but David, through song, comforted him.

David's experience reveals the truth that God's ways are always beyond our personal philosophies: " 'For My thoughts are not your thoughts, nor are your ways My ways,' says the LORD" (Isaiah 55:8). Not only are God's ways diverse, they are infinitely superior. David could afford to wait for God's timing. His life was in God's hands. As he trusted God for his elevation to the throne, David sang.

Even after he was comfortably enthroned over the twelve tribes of Israel, David continued his life of song: "I will sing to the LORD as long as I live; I will sing praise to my God while I have my being" (Psalm 104:33). He also admonished others to follow his example: "Sing to the LORD with the harp, with the harp and the sound of a psalm" (Psalm 98:5). Although singing had brought him into Saul's presence, David knew that a song to the Lord is infinitely more important because it is the surest route into the presence of the King of kings.

It has been the experience of many Christians that singing gives audience with the King. Released praise melodiously lifts our spirits and directs our energies to Jehovah. It also becomes a channel through which the spirit of faith can flow. Since, "... without faith it is impossible to please Him, for he who comes to God must believe that He is, and that He is a rewarder of those who diligently seek Him" (Hebrews 11:6), this song of faith becomes vital. It is our pass into God's presence. Even as David's first step to the throne was a song, so the first step in all worship should be song — "Sing to God, sing praises to His name; extol Him who rides on the clouds, by His name YAH, and rejoice before Him" (Psalm 68:4) — for praise through song brings us into God's presence.

Faith sings in the face of the enemy

Although David was very accustomed to singing and playing on his harp, playing before Saul was a new experience. Before, when he had sung unto Jehovah, his audience had primarily been sheep and, perhaps, heavenly angels. Now David was expected to sing with divine anointing in the courts of a willful and rejected king who was experiencing demonic activity. He soon learned what some of us now know: It is far easier to sing joyfully in the presence of the Lord than in the presence of any demonic being.

This shepherd lad had mastered the art of private devotions. He knew how to be spiritual in solitude. To be a successful leader of God's people, David also had to learn how to worship Jehovah in the company of others — particularly those who were not worshipers. To share the spiritual life that flows in worship, David had to worship around those who needed a touch of that life. As he moved from personal worship to public worship — from enjoying the life of God to ministering that life to others — David discovered that music is a marvelous vehicle for sharing a worship experience with others, for it can simultaneously minister unto God and minister God to others.

Saul did not need to be entertained. It is likely that he had court musicians and dancers for this purpose. Soulish music, however, could not reach this king because he was in a misery of spirit. David became valuable to Saul because his music touched Saul's tormented spirit.

David had already learned that all ministry will be tested. He had faced the threat of a bear and a lion while tending sheep. Why should he expect it to be easy to take authority over the spirit that troubled Saul? He later sang, "I will praise You with my whole heart; before the gods I will sing praises to You" (Psalm 138:1). The Hebrew word for "gods" refers to deities far lesser than Jehovah. It may refer either to kings of the earth or to demonic forces who seek to set themselves up as the rulers behind kings. David chose to ignore the demonic and to sing faith praises to Jehovah.

That this anointed singing was disturbing to the demons is a foregone conclusion, for David sang from a strong faith. The music of heaven is always disturbing to the forces of evil, but when the song of faith pierces the darkness in which they function, those forces react like a bull who has just been poked with an electric prod.

Before his death in 1969, the great English Bible teacher, Harold Horton, wrote in *The Gifts of the Spirit*,

> "Faith is the normal atmosphere of Heaven so difficult to acquire on earth because all Hell is against it. For by faith the weakest among us may storm the battlements of Hell and hurl the enemy from his challenging chariot."

If Rev. Horton was correct that "faith is the normal atmosphere of Heaven," then it becomes obvious that it would be an abnormal atmosphere on earth and a death-dealing atmosphere in hell. Just as a beam of light pierces the darkness, so faith dispels the energy of the satanic. The more brilliant the light, the more darkness it will disperse.

As David sang faith's song, it scattered the darkness in King Saul and allowed a measure of peace to return to his spirit: "And so it was, whenever the spirit from God was upon Saul, that David would take a harp and play it with his hand. Then Saul would become refreshed and well, and the distressing spirit would depart from him" (1 Samuel 16:23). The inner peace that David's singing brought to Saul so opened the heart of the king to this young shepherd boy that "he [Saul] loved him greatly, and he became his armorbearer" (1 Samuel 16:21).

Faith's song gives us favor

God works progressively in the lives of those who love Him. David did not step from shepherd to king in one motion. He was not qualified to make such a drastic step. Instead, he started walking up a staircase where each step became a learning experience.

David first came before Saul as a musician. His success in this role caused Saul to make him the king's armorbearer, or the private valet to the king: "Then Saul sent to Jesse, saying, 'Please let David stand before me, for he has found favor in my sight' " (1 Samuel 16:22). This position placed David in the palace permanently.

We should not be surprised, then, that wise King Solomon advised, "Whatever your hand finds to do, do it with your might ..." (Ecclesiastes 9:10) God tests us in the little things before trusting us with the larger things. Because David had passed the test as a singer, he could be promoted to more significant duties.

This principle is true in both the natural and the spiritual. A strong yearning for advancement is best furthered by a zealous application to today's tasks. Although we cannot earn the favor of God (His grace) — nor is it ever merited — every person mentioned in the Bible whom God chose for service was busy at a task. God doesn't choose the indolent. He chooses the industrious. Jesus declared, "He who is faithful in what is least is faithful also in much; and he who is unjust in what is least is unjust also in much (Luke 16:10).

Perhaps God was not seeking great, dynamic faith in David at this time; He was merely checking David's faith level. Giant-killing faith was not yet necessary, but faithfulness in song and in polishing the armor of the king was required. God seldomly tells us that He is giving us a test. He merely presents opportunities to us and watches our responses. David's faith responses to his obligations brought him into great favor with the very person who would tutor him for kingship.

Faith's song prevents jealousy

Neither Saul nor David understood God's plan for a teacher/student relationship between the two. Saul viewed David as his depression deterrent, and David filled his role as armorbearer as a routine public service. All the while, David was learning through the power of Saul's negative example.

David knew that he possessed the anointing for kingship. He also became increasingly aware that Saul had lost this anointing. Still, Saul had the very office for which God had anointed David. The potential for jealousy was strong. Many a church has been split when an associate pastor felt that he had a greater anointing than the senior pastor and made a political move to seat himself in the top position. Sometimes the senior pastor is unseated. At other times, the flock is split as the associate pastor takes part of the congregation and starts his own church.

We will never know if David toyed with such ideas. The Scriptures don't give even a slight hint of this type of attitude. David seemed to have a deep trust that God, who had called him, would place him on the throne at the proper time. "Trust in the Lord" is the repeated cry of David. From his experience David exclaimed: "Trust in the LORD, and do good; dwell in the land, and feed on His faithfulness. Delight yourself also in the LORD, and He shall give you the desires of your heart" (Psalm 37:3-4). "Trust in the LORD" is also the plea of the prophets and the exhortation of the epistles— "trust in the Lord forever" (Isaiah 26:4); — "trust ... in the living God" (1 Timothy 6:17).

What is there in God that is so specifically dependable or trustworthy that we dare embrace the exhortation of Peter: " ... casting all your care upon Him, for He cares for you" (1 Peter 5:7)? Like David, we can initially trust in God's self-existence, independence and eternity. He is before all things, being totally non-dependent upon anything outside of Himself. He is eternally existent. God will always be around when we need Him.

Second, we can learn with David that we can confide in and lean upon God's veracity and infallibility, for He is truth (see John 14:6). Therefore, every word He speaks is true. David was aware that Baalim had prophesied: "God is not a man, that He should lie ... " (Numbers 23:19) Thus, David relied upon God's word. If God said it, that settled it. We too must learn to accept God's Word as the final rule and authority of our lives.

Third, God was never a mere name to David. He counted on God's activity because he saw God energetically working for His people. Thus, David learned that God is not only able, He is active. We too can join David in confidently depending on God's omnipotence and activity. There is no limit to His ability to do all things. The great doxology of the Book of Ephesians proclaims, "Now to Him who is able to do *exceedingly abundantly above* all that we ask or think ..." (Ephesians 3:20) God was, and is, the source and sustainer of life.

Because David could trust in the living God, he did not need to be jealous of the reigning king. David was confident that "... He who [hath] begun a good work in [him would] complete it until the day of Jesus Christ" (Philippians 1:6). David could rest in God instead of trying to take the kingdom from Saul. Faith's song kept David focused on God rather than on God's promises.

Faith's song gives form to faith

Out of his experience that began as a court musician and included his subsequent promotion to an armorbearer, David sang, "Commit your way to the LORD, trust also in Him, and He shall bring it to pass" (Psalm 37:5). The Hebrew word for "commit" here is *gaal*, "to roll," which is often translated "trust," while the word used for "trust" is *bathach*, which means "to flee for refuge." David literally says, "Roll your way upon the Lord; flee to Him for refuge; and He shall bring it to pass." David knew and could sing that God, who is always trustworthy, has created us as trusting, dependent persons. Rather than fight for what was to be his, David learned to flow with it.

The sweet singer of Israel learned that trust is the first fruit of faith. He understood that it is impossible to please God without faith, but he also perceived that without trust it was impossible for God to please David. If faith was the energy by which David took a step in God, trust had to be the rest by which he stood on God and His Word. Faith originates in God. Our response to faith is trust.

David joyfully sang of his trust in God and of the God in whom He trusted. This song of faith not only gave expression to his faith, it also gave a positive form to that faith. When he melodiously vocalized his trust, David better visualized his faith. One verse of his song goes: "... I trust in the mercy of God forever and ever" (Psalm 52:8), while another verse says, "He has put a new song in my mouth — praise to our God; many will see it and fear, and will trust in the Lord" (Psalm 40:3). When the song of faith gives form to that faith, it gives others something to stand upon. It also helps them to trust in God with David.

Chapter 3

David Defined His Faith

Faith's Nature

Perhaps only the poets and the prophets are permitted to give animating life to nature, but the years I have spent along the Columbia River have caused me to view this magnificent body of water as being very much alive. If it had an intellect that could communicate, we might hear the small spring at the headwaters sigh a relief of satisfaction as it flowed into Columbia Lake near the crest of the Rocky Mountains. Security at last! But before long, the call of the ocean would become overwhelming.

If inanimate objects can have "faith," this stream of water demonstrates it. It faces a vast unknown with many natural and man-made hindrances, but it must serve the purpose for which it was created, for this is its only way of worshiping the Creator. This water was not created to stagnate in a basin. It is destined to flow 1,214 miles into the Pacific Ocean at Astoria, Oregon. It has done just that for thousands of years.

All nature has "faith" to fulfill the purpose for which God created it. However, God has endowed people with such an intellect that they frequently doubt their ability to function according to God's plan. God has declared to men and women: "... He who has begun a good work in you will complete it until the day of Jesus Christ" (Philippians 1:6). God never starts something He is unable to complete. When a person can embrace what God has said as truth, faith replaces fear and God's designed purpose begins to function.

The Scriptures clearly declare that David was chosen, called and commissioned by God to be king over all Israel. Although David quickly embraced that choice and answered the call, the route to the throne was barricaded with hindrances, obstructions and detours. David promptly discovered that the way up was often down. Long before he became the leader of God's people, he endured years of isolation, privation and rejection. Instead of the palace, he lived in caves. His only army was a rag-tag coalition of outlaws and runaway slaves. Many doubted that he would ever get to the throne, but David was convinced that what God had promised, He was able to perform. David's faith maintained and strengthened him. He could never have made it without that faith.

David demonstrated *true faith*

I have never met a Bible scholar who denied the abundant faith that flowed through David's life. Even casual reading shows that his faith was genuine. What Paul wrote of Timothy could have been written of David: "... I call to remembrance the genuine faith that is in you, which dwelt first in your grandmother Lois and your mother Eunice, and I am persuaded is in you also" (2 Timothy 1:5). Three successive generations possessed true faith, or as other translators have put it: "unalloyed" (Berkeley), "unqualified" (Amplified) and "unhypocritical" (Wuest) faith.

David's faith pleased God and moved His hand on behalf of the king because it was faith that was undisguised and without hypocrisy. Counterfeit faith is never accepted in Heaven's bank. But what is genuine faith?

Faith is a New Testament word that was totally unknown to David. It comes from the Greek word *pistis*, which primarily means "a firm persuasion" or "a conviction based upon hearing." Far from exhausting the meaning of the word *faith*, these definitions merely indicate the normal usage in the Greek. Others have added their views to this definition through the years. Dr. John Erskine, for instance, defined faith by declaring, "It is, in general, an assent to the word of God, in which there is a light, a glory, a brightness, which believers, and they only, perceive."

That David received this light and glory seems obvious from his songs, for he sang: "The LORD is my light and my salvation; whom shall I fear? The LORD is the strength of my life; of whom shall I be afraid?" (Psalm 27:1) "For with You is the fountain of life; in Your light we see light" (Psalm 36:9).

The basic Bible definition for faith is found in the Book of Hebrews: "Now faith is the substance of things hoped for, the evidence of things not seen" (Hebrews 11:1). Faith is the foundation upon which all the things we hope for find support. It becomes the initial evidence of God's unseen promises. Perhaps it is unfair to call faith either an attitude or an energy, but it controls our attitudes and channels the energy of God's Word into our day-by-day walk with God.

David lived too early to hear the Bible call faith — "*precious* faith" (2 Peter 1:1) and "*holy* faith" (Jude 20) — but his lifestyle proves that he viewed its value as priceless and its virtue as peerless. He knew that any attempt to fake a precious and holy faith was automatically doomed to failure from the very start, for the crass hypocrisy behind such pretense would preclude a holy result anyway.

During the years that David served God in public life, he saw that mental assent, emotional stirrings and misdirected zeal were often substituted for true faith, but when the test came, these expedients always failed. No matter how strong the emotions or how fervent the zeal, they never metamorphosed into faith any more than an incubated hen's egg ever produced a calf. This sweet singer of Israel discovered that man's soulish nature and God's divine faith are distinct and separate. Neither can be transformed into the other.

From David's point of view, the greatest tragedy of pretended faith is the total needlessness of it. Divine faith is abundantly available, thereby nullifying the need for spurious faith. Faith flows when God speaks, for God Himself is the source of our faith, and His quickened word is the channel through which that faith is transmitted to others. Many generations after David, the apostle Paul wrote: "So then faith comes by hearing, and hearing by the word of God" (Romans 10:17). God has never been known to have a shortage of faith, but men have been known to be deficient in their hearing of the voice of God, thereby depleting their faith. Because David was a consistent communicator with God who learned to be a good listener, his life demonstrates faith in action.

True, pure, divine faith is God's ultimate desire for each of our lives. Holy, precious faith that is unadulterated, undisguised, unalloyed, unqualified and without hypocrisy is God's never-changing goal for His Church and every member in it.

David may not have had the word *faith* in his vocabulary, but he had this force at work in his life. None of our modern definitions of faith seem to have occurred to him, but the power of faith continually worked for him. He tended to refer to it as dependence, confidence, trust and hope. None of these were false in the life of King David.

Among the greatest reasons for false faith is a weak understanding of the manifold and magnificently varied facets that make up divine faith. Possibly we've tried to bake our "faith cake" with too few ingredients. If so, the cause of failure is self-evident. To have success in the life of faith, a proper blend of all the necessary ingredients is required. David seemed to have his ingredients blended perfectly.

David defined his faith as *dependence*

In the precious psalm where David speaks of the LORD as forgiving iniquities, healing diseases, redeeming life and crowning us with lovingkindness and tender mercies, David says: "As a father pities his children, so the LORD pities those who fear Him" (Psalm 103:13). David had a father concept of God and he developed a loving relationship with this Father. That this was both designed by God and a delight to God is evident, for in speaking of David, God said, "I have found My servant David; with My holy oil I have anointed him ... He shall cry to Me, 'You are my Father, my God, and the rock of my salvation' " (Psalm 89:20,26). David leaned upon the Lord in total dependence, much as his children looked to him for support, protection and provision.

David's early concept of faith was relational. In his youth, he functioned out of this relationship in killing the lion and the bear that threatened the lambs in the flock. When explaining his ability to kill them with his bare hands, he said: "'The LORD ... delivered me from the paw of the lion and from the paw of the bear ...'" (1 Samuel 17:37) Later, when Goliath threatened the armies of Israel, David volunteered to meet the giant in one-on-one combat because "the LORD, who delivered me from the paw of the lion and from the paw of the bear, He will deliver me from the hand of this Philistine.' And Saul said to David, 'Go, and the LORD be with you!' " (1 Samuel 17:37) Just as a child is fearless when he is in the company of a loving father, so David was confident and fearless whenever he was aware of the presence of Jehovah.

We would call this faith in New Testament terminology.

True faith comes only from God. Jesus said, "Have faith *in* God," and, "Have the faith *of* God." God is both the object and the source of our faith. The more intimate our relationship with God is, the more our faith will flow. David's greatest exploits of faith followed times of fellowship with Jehovah. He knew that "Daddy" could do anything.

David was a man of action. His concept of life seemed to be, "If it is worth doing, do it yesterday." Yet there were many circumstances when he disciplined himself to wait for God to intervene. He refused to kill King Saul on the two or more opportunities when, from a human viewpoint, it was the logical thing to do. David was assured that God would dispose of Saul in His own way, in His own time.

David's desire to wait for God's leading is also evident in his military leadership. Before several of his battles, David inquired of the Lord whether or not he should attack the enemy. He always waited for God's instructions, for he realized that until he had a direct word from the Lord, he had no basis for faith.

In his more mature years, David sang, "Rest in the LORD, and wait patiently for Him; do not fret because of him who prospers in his way, because of the man who brings wicked schemes to pass" (Psalm 37:7). He had learned that "Daddy knows best." Because of this, David not only functioned in faith, he rested in faith. To David, his Father God was not only "the LORD ... a man of war" (Exodus 15:3) but also "the Prince of Peace" (Isaiah 9:6). If God wasn't warring, David remained home and ruled his kingdom in peace and righteousness with the same faith and confidence with which he battled.

In the years of old age, David exulted: "Because You have been my help, therefore in the shadow of Your wings I will rejoice" (Psalm 63:7). Throughout the years of running from Saul and of conquering Israel's enemies, David found shelter and protection under the shadow of God's wings. Like the mother hen protecting her chicks from an attacking hawk by enfolding her offspring under her outspread wings, God had repeatedly pulled David close to the divine heart by offering protection, shelter and comfort to His servant. In retrospect, David said that this was a basic cause for his rejoicing.

During the period when I wrote this chapter, I had the experience of sitting with a pastor and his wife, nibbling on a sandwich, when their three-year-old daughter came walking into the kitchen declaring in her most melodious voice, "I'm happy. I'm happy!" There was no apparent reason for this for she had received no gift nor had a promise been extended to her. She was just happy in the security of the love in that home and in the fact that her parents were in the room with her. This was the way David felt. He, too, was conscious of God's presence, for he wrote: "The LORD is near to all who call upon Him, to all who call upon Him in truth" (Psalm 145:18). The warmth of the Father's love made him sing, "I'm happy! I'm happy! In the shadow of Your wings I will rejoice."

David defined his faith as *hope*

During the years that David served King Saul as a private valet, he knew that the kingly anointing rested upon David, not Saul. When Saul began to realize this, he sought to kill David to preserve the kingly line for his son Jonathan, but David fled for his life into the wilderness areas of the kingdom. David had a promise. Even when faith seemed unable to appropriate that promise and bring it into fulfilled fact, David continued to hope anyway. Hope outwaited his faith, and the interim was an opportunity to develop stronger faith.

David could sing out of a wealth of experience: "Be of good courage, and He shall strengthen your heart, all you who hope in the LORD" (Psalm 31:24). Isn't faith a strengthening of the heart? David said that strong hope in the Lord will energize this strength. It has been pointed out that animals are known to die quickly when experiencing hopelessness and to revive quickly when given new hope. There is also medical evidence that helplessness and hopelessness can contribute to the development of organic disease in people. When hope vanishes, life vegetates. So Samuel Johnson was right when he observed that where there is no hope, there can be no endeavor. Three times the psalmist wrote, "Why are you cast down, O my soul? And why are you disquieted within me? *Hope in God* ..." (Psalms 42:5,11 and 43:5) The loss of hope is the loss of strong desire and burning expectation. It results in despondency, gloominess and apathy.

While hope is not the only activating and guiding principle in a person's life, it is a major factor affecting all other principles, for nothing spurs one to action without some measure of hope or certainty that his or her action will satisfy or fulfill the person in one way or another. Paul listed hope as one of the three eternal graces that are now active in men's lives. He wrote: "And now abide faith, hope, love, these three ..." (1 Corinthians 13:13), contrasting "abide" with the "will fail ... cease ... vanish away" of verse eight. Charles Spurgeon said, "In the garden of hope grow the laurels for future victories, the roses of coming joy, the lilies of approaching peace." Hope gives beauty and courage to the period of life between the promise and its performance.

The *New English Bible* offers the following translation for Colossians 1:4-5:

... we have heard of the faith you hold in Christ Jesus, and the love you bear towards all God's people. Both spring from the hope stored up for you in heaven — that hope of which you learned when the message of the true Gospel first came to you.

In my book *Let Us See Jesus* I comment:

"Faith and love both spring from hope. It is almost as though Paul visualized hope as a gushing fountain of pure water atop a tall mountain. Some of this water flowed down one side of the mountain, eventually forming a river of faith, while the rest of the water flowed down the opposite side of the mountain, forming a mighty stream of love, but although both streams flowed in different directions, each had its source in the same fountain. Hope is the fountainhead from which both faith and love flow. It is the quality from which faith springs and the atmosphere in which love grows. It is the Christian hope within us that fosters and ferments faith and love which flow out of us."

This interconnection between faith and hope is seen in the basic biblical definition for faith: "Faith is the substance of things hoped for, the evidence of things not seen" (Hebrews 11:1). Faith is not the hope that looks forward with wistful longing; it is the hope that looks forward with utter certainty. This hope will not take refuge in a "perhaps," for it is founded on a conviction.

Faith and hope are very much like a hand and a glove. Although they are complementary, they are not truly interchangeable. *Hope* is based on desires, facts and rational considerations. *Faith*, on the other hand, is based not only on such facts and considerations but on a sense of God's presence in one's own life; it is greatly strengthened by one's personal devotion and commitment to Christ. It is in faith that Christ Himself becomes one's hope.

David did not have the word *faith* in his vocabulary, but his hope was vibrant and deeply involved in a personal relationship with Jehovah. Thus he wrote: "Behold, the eye of the LORD is on those who fear Him, on those who hope in His mercy" (Psalm 33:18). "For in You, O LORD, I hope; You will hear, O Lord my God" (Psalm 38:15). Like many believers who lived both before and after him, David functioned in a living faith without defining it in New Testament terms. What he called *hope* often moved into the realm of *faith*, because he reached into the unseen and grasped the object of his hope, bringing it into the reality of his current existence.

David's hope undergirded him with ceaseless joy and strengthened him in patient doing and suffering. The years he spent fleeing from Saul were not all wretched and fearsome. Some of his most victorious psalms were written during this time. While hiding for his life in the cave, he sang:

My heart is steadfast, O God, my heart is steadfast; I will sing and give praise. Awake, my glory! Awake, lute and harp! I will awaken the dawn. I will praise You, O Lord, among the peoples; I will sing to You among the nations. For Your mercy reaches unto the heavens, and Your truth unto the clouds. Be exalted, O God, above the heavens; let Your glory be above all the earth (Psalm 57:7-11).

This is not the song of a hopeless person. It is vibrantly alive with the faith that Jehovah is able to do what He has promised. It sings victoriously in the midst of extremely negative circumstances. Indeed, this psalm reveals that David discovered what Paul asked the Christians in Rome to learn: to be "rejoicing in hope, patient in tribulation, continuing steadfastly in prayer" (Romans 12:12). Hope spurs faith to song. Actually, hope, when connected with faith, is only a baby step from trust, and *trust* is the Old Testament equivalent for the New Testament word *faith*.

David defined his faith as *trust*

Trust is not a product of fear; it is a preventive of fear. Trust is not a response to a circumstance; it is a result of a relationship.

I was flying to Miami, Florida on a flight that seemed to stop at every other airport on the route. In the row in front of me, an aging man began to scream in terror as we made our first landing approach. The stewardess tried unsuccessfully to calm him and, in desperation, fastened him in his seat with a loud command to "shut up!"

Since there was a vacant seat next to him, I moved up beside him and introduced myself. I explained that I was a pilot and fully understood everything that was happening. Taking his hand, I explained every change of sound and movement of the plane.

He told me that he was 91 and this was his first plane ride. By the second landing, he was enjoying himself so much that he stood to his feet and shouted, "This is wonderful." Returning to his seat, he told me, "If I ever take another plane trip, I hope you are on it with me. You've taken all the fear of flying from me."

David cried, "Whenever I am afraid, I will trust in You" (Psalm 56:3). No matter how storm-tossed his life became, David was confident that his God was in charge of the operation. The *Merriam-Webster Dictionary* defines trust as "assured reliance on the character, strength or truth of someone or something" and lists "confidence" and "dependence" as synonyms. David, then, was saying, "I will have an assured reliance on the character, strength and truth of Almighty God, and I will not be afraid."

The word *trust* is used over 140 times in the Old Testament, while it appears in the New Testament but 40 times. New Testament writers prefer the word *faith*. Even though the eleventh chapter of Hebrews credits many Old Testament characters with faith, the Old Testament speaks of their *trusting* in God. They were men and women whose confident reliance upon God radically affected their attitudes and actions in life. It is not so much that they were people to be trusted — although with our hindsight we can affirm that they actually were — but that they were people who trusted in God. David is among those listed in this chapter.

Trust is inherent in our nature, for life would be impossible without it. How long has it been since you saw someone thoroughly examine a chair before sitting in it? No, we are not without trust, for in many ways we are very trusting creatures. The redemption or the ruination that our trust brings to us hinges on the object of our trust. In what or in whom do we trust? Paul declares, "... we should not trust in ourselves but in God who raises the dead" (2 Corinthians 1:9).

Dwight L. Moody is quoted as having said, "Trust in yourself, and you are doomed to disappointment; trust in your friends, and they will die and leave you; trust in reputation, and some slanderous tongue may blast it; but trust in God, and you are never to be confounded in time or eternity."

"Trust in the Lord" (Psalm 37:3) is a frequent phrase in David's songs. To trust is to confide in God as our most trusted friend and to lean on Him as our strongest supporter. David knew that he could trust in God's self-existence, independence and eternity. He would always be around when David needed Him. David also learned that he could confide in and lean upon Jehovah's veracity and infallibility, for He is the truth (see John 14:6). Therefore, every word He speaks is true. David was aware that Baalim had prophesied that "God is not a man, that He should lie" (Numbers 23:19). David discovered that everything God said to him came to pass. No wonder that he lived his life with the motto: "If God said it, that settles it." God's Word was the final rule and authority of his life.

In his confident trust in God, David depended on God's omnipotence and activity. He believed implicitly that there is no limit to Jehovah's ability to do. He equally believed that God was active in doing what He was able to do. He did not visualize God as a mere name. He knew Jehovah to be energetic on behalf of His people. David saw God as the source and sustainer of his life.

David also trusted with hope in God's expressed love and availability. He found that God was not only love by nature, but that He consistently expressed that love to him, even as He makes that love unceasingly available to all. David fled to this refuge repeatedly.

David correctly associated a knowledge of God with trust in God. He wrote: "And those who know Your name will put their trust in You; for You, LORD, have not forsaken those who seek You" (Psalm 9:10). David functioned in neither blind faith nor blind trust. The more he knew God, the more he found God to be trustworthy. Trust is built not merely on the promises of God but upon the person of God, for no promise is greater than the one who makes that promise.

I heard Paul Johanson, a personal friend of mine, say in a sermon: "Trust is the first fruit of faith.

Without faith it is impossible to please God; without trust it is impossible for God to please us. Faith is the energy by which I take a step in God; trust is the rest by which I stand on God and His Word. Faith originates in God; my response is trust." I think David's life agrees with this.

David evidenced a trust that God would do what was best because of who He is, even in the absence of a specific word. Thus, he could affirm: "But as for me, I trust in You, O LORD; I say, 'You are my God' " (Psalm 31:14). "The LORD is my rock and my fortress and my deliverer; my God, my strength, in whom I will trust; my shield and the horn of my salvation, my stronghold" (Psalm 18:2). He was consistently aware of the true object of his trust, and he focused on Him.

Chapter 4

David Focused His Faith

Faith's Object

All who have been around the Columbia River know that it sings as it flows. Sometimes it is like a quiet lullaby as it glides gently through wide stretches. At other times, it is almost like a militant march as it rushes through confining gorges. Its roar can be deafening as it pours over the spillways of dams, but the song never ceases.

David's life was never without a song. Its cadence varied and its melody changed, but it consistently spoke of David's complete trust and absolute confidence in Jehovah. His earliest song has become his most popular, for it undergirded his entire career from shepherd to king. Whether warring as a soldier, working as a king, or worshiping as a saint, David confidently sang:

The LORD is my shepherd; I shall not want. He makes me to lie down in green pastures; He leads me beside the still waters. He restores my soul; He leads me in the paths of righteousness for His name's sake. Yea, though I walk through the valley of the shadow of death, I will fear no

evil; for You are with me; Your rod and Your staff,
they comfort me. You prepare a table before me in
the presence of my enemies; You anoint my head
with oil; my cup runs over. Surely goodness and
mercy shall follow me all the days of my life; and
I will dwell in the house of the LORD forever
(Psalm 23).

David learned to focus his faith on the Lord in every
circumstance of life.

David focused his faith on God's *person*

David's song began, "The LORD is my shepherd."
David knew that the nature of the shepherd sets the
standard for the life of the sheep. A caring shepherd
meets the needs of the sheep, while a selfish shepherd
seeks to have the sheep meet his needs. David never
feared that God looked upon him as lamb chops or
mutton. He viewed God as the source of all necessary
things in life. He wrote: "The LORD is my strength and
my shield; my heart trusted in Him, and I am helped;
therefore my heart greatly rejoices, and with my song
I will praise Him" (Psalm 28:7).

Many fail to see that the ultimate object of their
faith is God Himself, which causes some to prostitute
their faith rather than progress in it. David seemed to
recognize that the measurement of faith is not only its
strength but its object.

It is possible to have faith in faith. Some have almost deified faith, believing that their faith can do all
things, provide all things, and solve all mysteries. Perhaps the resurgence in this twentieth century of
ascribing Godlike qualities to faith, instead of letting
faith bring us to God, is the result of America's
wholesale embracing of the philosophy of humanism,
which puts man at the center of all things instead of
God. Whenever we espouse the deity of man, we automatically forsake the deity of God. Consequently, we

subconsciously think of faith as a force we can possess that will, of itself, produce or perform whatever we direct it to do. David viewed faith as a channel to bring persons into a walk with God, who the Scriptures affirm is to be the object of our faith.

David did not fall into the trap of having faith in formulas more than having faith in God and His Word. Today's scientifically oriented society is formula oriented. We love to bring the exactness of mathematical equations into our religious experiences and we tend to deal with phrases, texts (sometimes out of context), cliches and specific recipes in preference to dealing with the living God.

David knew that it is not a formula, but faith, that is pleasing to God. God sometimes follows a known formula, but oftentimes, in His omniscience, He functions beyond our limited, finite understanding of His principles, power and purposes. As we have seen, David did not rely upon a formula when he faced Goliath. He said: " 'The LORD, who delivered me from the paw of the lion and from the paw of the bear, He will deliver me from the hand of this Philistine.' And Saul said to David, 'Go, and the LORD be with you!' " (1 Samuel 17:37) This was just another way for David to sing, "The Lord is my Shepherd." Nothing was too difficult for Jehovah.

David seemed to know that when we shift the focus of our faith from God to anything else, we tend to think and exercise faith *for* rather than faith *in*. He did not declare his faith *for* victory over Goliath. He declared his faith *in* Jehovah.

A "faith *for*" mentality makes us the source; our possessions become the object and our faith is viewed as the force that brings the desired thing or end into our experience. In a subtle way, we seek to become the creators rather than the creatures who have access to the Creator. David felt that God's ultimate purpose for giving us faith was to make us dependent upon Him, not independent from Him.

David focused his faith on God's *provision*

Because he was comfortable in God's person, David rested securely in God's provision. His heart sang: "I shall not want" (Psalm 23:1). He was convinced that "... no good thing will He withhold from those who walk uprightly" (Psalm 84:11). Sheep with a good shepherd never lack provision, and David was convinced that Jehovah is the Good Shepherd. Jesus said of Himself, "I am the good shepherd. The good shepherd gives His life for the sheep" (John 10:11). Such a caring shepherd provides for the needs of the sheep long before they are aware they have a need. For David, it was a case of, "It shall come to pass that before they call, I will answer; and while they are still speaking, I will hear" (Isaiah 65:24).

"He makes me to lie down in green pastures," David's song continued. Because he was a shepherd, David knew that sheep will not sleep in their food supply unless they are forced to do so. David's sheep had such an abundance of food that they did not have to leave it for the barren places to sleep. They could lie down in the midst of the lush pasture, knowing that there was plenty more available. Likewise, David did not feel the need to hoard God's provisions; he had the faith to believe that he could live off God's perpetual supply.

"He leads me beside the still waters" was David's vocalization of the many times he had briefly dammed up flowing streams that disturbed the peace of his sheep and made quiet puddles from which they could drink. He knew that his God would not only provide what he needed, but that He would give it to him in such a manner that he could respond positively.

When we channel faith directly to God's person, we find that faith in God also involves faith in God's provisions. We, with David, learn that God is not only able to do, He has provided to do. David knew that Israel had lived for forty years in God's *provision* of manna, not in His promise of manna or His demonstrated ability to produce that manna. God, our loving heavenly Father, has made lavish provision for His children. We do not need to lack any good thing, nor do we need to resort to great pleadings or the expenditure of excessive spiritual energy to receive God's provisions. When we are seated at the Father's table, we only need to say, "Pass the potatoes, please." God's supplies are always available to us because He instructs us: "Ask, and it will be given to you ..." (Matthew 7:7)

Faith for provision, apart from faith in God's person, becomes extremely difficult because Christ Jesus is God's provision for His people. He testified: "I am the way ..." (John 14:6) God has not provided for us apart from Himself, so true faith will be more than an intelligent understanding. It will be a deliberate commitment to a Person. Faith involves us with a Person, not an impersonal power. If my wife goes on a trip by herself, she seeks money for her ticket, food and lodging; but if she goes with me, she comfortably expects me to be her source of provision and merely stays close to me at meal times. Should it be any less in our relationship with God? It wasn't with David.

David focused his faith on God's *purposes*

When the shepherd lad sang, "He restores my soul; He leads me in the paths of righteousness for His name's sake," he was singing his faith in God's purposes. The soul that had been so marred and defiled by sin was being restored to the purposes God had intended when He created mankind, so that God's people would " ... all have one shepherd; they shall also walk in My judgments and observe My statutes, and do them" (Ezekiel 37:24).

David sensed that God imparts faith to persons to bring them close to Himself, for God made us to have intimate fellowship, union and communion with Him. Although sin separates men and women from God, salvation has reunited the creature with the Creator, and faith is the divine channel of both salvation and companionship. David knew this from experience, for after his sin with Bathsheba, he repentently cried, "Restore to me the joy of Your salvation, and uphold me with Your generous Spirit" (Psalm 51:12).

David wanted more than mere forgiveness or the release from punishment. His yearning, burning passion was for a fresh relationship with God. Knowing God was paramount on his priority list. Motivating, manipulating or moving God on his behalf did not enter into David's concept of faith, for the Almighty God was the consistent object of his faith.

Dare we be content with a lesser knowing? Is it satisfying to God for us to be so enamored with the power of faith and what it will produce that we fail to be deeply in love with Him, the true source and object of our faith?

Without faith, God can be neither appreciated nor apprehended, for "without faith it is impossible to please Him, for he who comes to God must believe that He is, and that He is a rewarder of those who diligently seek Him" (Hebrews 11:6). God cannot be discovered by persons; He must reveal Himself to them. Faith is the vital key that unlocks the door to the knowledge of God. To seek God apart from faith is to seek in vain, but "you will seek Me and find Me, when you search for Me with all your heart" (Jeremiah 29:13).

David knew that the successful search for God is a search of the heart because faith is a matter of the heart, not of the head. Faith, when released from our restraints, ascends toward God's presence as naturally as a gas-filled balloon rises when its string is released. Perhaps, if we would cease grasping our faith so tightly and just relax in the faith that God has given to us, we would find ourselves being lifted into His presence as freely and repeatedly as David was.

David loosely knew that God's purposes for his life included being king of Israel, but he was a fugitive from Saul for many years. Because David's faith was anchored in God and His purposes, he never waivered from the inner conviction that he would, indeed, rule over Israel without any manipulation on his part to make God's promise a reality. David trusted in God to perform His word, and God did everything He had said, and far more.

David focused his faith on God's *protection*

It is not by accident that this man who worshiped with a fervent faith included a verse in his song that says: "Yea, though I walk through the valley of the shadow of death, I will fear no evil; for You are with me; Your rod and Your staff, they comfort me" (Psalm 23:4). Being a person of faith does not immunize one from fear. David learned very early in his life that fear and faith will not mix. Fear says, "It won't be done," while faith says, "It shall be done." David could not be filled with anxiety over his tomorrow and still be filled with confidence in the God who holds tomorrow. The energy that once flowed to God as trust would, instead, flow to negative circumstances as terror.

David learned that a walk of faith has its enemies. Probably the greatest opposition to faith is fear. Unbelief, considered by some to be faith's greatest enemy, is simply the absence of faith. Fear is faith moving in the wrong direction. It is a confidence in the opposite of what God has spoken. In the realm of the demonic, fear is to demons what faith is to God — a commitment of your belief in their power. That is why demons consistently seek to produce terror. They receive greater authority and ability to work in the lives and affairs of those who fear them. Fear is tacit permission for them to function.

Because faith is so vital to our entering into a continual relationship with God, fear cannot be present. Somehow we innately fear the unknown. Almost every time an angel appeared to a person in the New Testament, the angel's first words had to be "Fear not." The sight of a creature from God's Kingdom produced fear, not faith. Jesus even had to calm the fear of His disciples after He performed the miracle of the prodigious catch of fish (see Luke 5:10). It seems that no matter what level our faith may have attained, when we are confronted by anything beyond that level, our initial response is fear. What is meant to produce faith within us is channeled into the opposite direction, and it becomes fear.

David seemed to realize that fear and faith are diametrically opposed to each other. Fear deprives a person of reason, while faith gives a reason. Fear terrorizes; faith stabilizes. Fear excites the human nature, but faith calms a person better than any medicinal tranquilizer. Fear brings sickness; faith brings health. Fear causes insanity, while faith gives people sound minds. There just is no common ground on which fear and faith can rest. That is why David sang, "I will fear no evil."

David rejected this fear response. Even when he was walking in the valley of death's shadow, he refused to fear the presence of an evil force. His faith was focused on "You are with me." The smallest child is comforted in the presence of a loving father.

Today we hear a great deal about having faith for things. Some even go so far as to categorize their faith, declaring that they have "healing faith," "saving faith," "faith for finances," "faith for business dealings," and so on. This makes about as much sense as saying that we have "refrigerating electricity" or "vacuuming electricity." In their very definitions of faith, those who categorize their faith declare that things are the focus of their faith. This focus is completely contrary to the Bible, because the Bible calls for the Lord to be the object of our faith. One faith — the faith of God — is sufficient to meet all our needs if we keep God as the true focus of that faith.

There is no greater unknown to the believer than death. We only know what God has told us about it. David came to realize that faith is basically believing the word of another and accepting the unseen as real. Thus, faith moves into that unseen, making it become a fact, and the reward of faith is seeing what we believed. That which faith has seen and touched becomes as real to the believer as that which his natural eyes have seen and his human hands have handled. Because of this, David could walk with loved ones in death's shadow without fear. His faith in God accepted what God says about life beyond the grave.

In our scientific age, many people draw away from accepting anything by faith, saying that it is neither rational nor scientific. Yet most major scientific breakthroughs started as an unproven premise that someone believed enough to act on. Long before they could prove it in a test tube or by a computer, they saw it by faith.

In the spiritual world, God declares as truth that which doesn't harmonize with facts as we know them in our human world. Faith lays hold upon God's declaration, not because it understands it, but because it has reason to believe the speaker — God. By reaching into the unseen world through faith, the reality of what God said becomes demonstrable. Like David, we too need not fear evil, even when walking between the two worlds.

David understood that terrorizing fear prevents worship. We too must learn that lesson until we can see beyond the fear that assails us when the devil interrupts our devotions with a challenge to our worthiness to love and be loved by so exalted a being as God, and we find ourselves asking, "How dare I think that He is my Beloved, and that I am His?" God is neither pleased nor served when we fear His majesty in a terrorized manner. When John the Beloved, on the Isle of Patmos, fell at the feet of Jesus in terror, he was told: "Do not be afraid ..." (Revelation 1:17)

Like David, we need to learn the balance of letting the Lord be glorious to us, yet near to us. We do well to exalt Him upon the throne, but we must remember that we are seated with Him on that throne. While meditating on His perfection, we should remember that He has perfection of mercy as well as of holiness. Do not fear to love, relate to, and enjoy the Lord. David didn't. Our safety lies in trusting Jesus and refusing to be afraid of Him. No soul has been saved or delivered by being afraid of Christ, just as no prodigal will find forgiveness by being afraid of his father.

David focused his faith on God's *preparation*

When David sang: "You prepare a table before me in the presence of my enemies; You anoint my head with oil; my cup runs over" (Psalm 23:5), he was focusing his faith on God's advance preparation for his life. David knew from experience that while the sheep rested in today's pasture, the shepherd walked through tomorrow's pasture removing everything that would be unsafe. The table he sang of was a tall rock on which the shepherd placed all the poisonous weeds and thorns that would hurt the sheep. The sheep could graze safely because the shepherd had made advance preparations for them.

Later in life when David faced some critical circumstances, his focused faith in God's provision lifted him above fear into faith. Faith is despised when we fear in the midst of a desperate situation. There is no such thing as a hopeless case when we entrust the matter into the care of Jehovah. Much of life is beyond our control, but nothing in our puny little lives is ever beyond His capacity. Fearing inflation will not make it subside any more than worrying about recession will turn the economy around. It is not fear but faith that changes the events in our lives from poverty to plenty, and from failure to success. Likewise, faith, not fear, prompts the hand of God to move on behalf of His troubled children.

When Joshua stood with the Lord on the mountain looking into the Promised Land, God told him, "... Be strong and of good courage; do not be afraid, nor be dismayed ..." (Joshua 1:9) Like Joshua and David, we are not only commanded to give no place to fear but we are also exhorted to make much room for courage, because courage is a holding pattern for faith. Courage, God's positive replacement for the negative of fear, is a source of strength for all believers. Therefore, David exhorted: "Be of good courage, and He shall strengthen your heart, all you who hope in the LORD" (Psalm 31:24).

Following Christ is not without its difficulties. Life in His footsteps requires us to endure moral conflicts, to engage in spiritual warfare and to strive against sin. Courage is God's provision that enables us to endure the reverses and the sufferings that result from such actions. This courage that God demands of His children does not come by looking inward, but by looking upward.

By focusing his faith on the God of provision, David took courage in the most negative situations. He relied on his Shepherd's care to remove those things that were life-threatening and to anoint him with oil when he became wounded. David's dependency upon God's loving concern never faltered from youth to old age. He believed that God never promised anything unless He had already had made the necessary preparations to provide it.

David focused his faith on God's *perpetuity*

David believed that God was an eternal God who dwelt in eternity. He looked for the eternal value in everything connected with Jehovah, as revealed in the conclusion of his shepherd song: "Surely goodness and mercy shall follow me all the days of my life; and I will dwell in the house of the LORD forever" (Psalm 23:6). Therefore, David's faith was not focused entirely on the "sweet by and by." He fervently trusted that God could and would work in the nasty "here and now." He did not fear to lose temporary blessings because He expected goodness and mercy to perpetually follow him as long as he lived. Although his faith reached up to God for a beginning point of blessing, he refused to see an end to that operation. Consequently, He wrote: "Save Your people, and bless Your inheritance; shepherd them also, and bear them up forever" (Psalm 28:9). True shepherd that he was, David viewed the flock as a perpetual thing. Sheep came and sheep went, but the flock remained. David expected God's dealings with His inheritance to have this same perpetuity.

David's faith projected his worship beyond the present into the future, for he worshiped an eternal God, and he knew that he, himself, possessed eternal life. In a song dedicated to the chief musician, David wrote,

> *I will abide in Your tabernacle forever ... You will prolong the king's life, his years as many generations. He shall abide before God forever. Oh, prepare mercy and truth, which may preserve him! So I will sing praise to Your name forever, that I may daily perform my vows* (Psalm 61:4,6-8).

The now and the forever were interrelated in David's worship. He would sing forever, but he daily performed his vows. His faith worked in the present, but he viewed eternity as a reality. Because his faith was correctly focused, David anticipated no interruption in his worship of Jehovah — even though he realized that there would come a change of the location from which he worshiped. He would worship either with the saints below or with the saints above. But the same God would receive his worship and give him blessings. Whether that worship involved ritual sacrifices, rejoicing songs or recited supplications, David envisioned perpetuity in his actions.

Chapter 5

David Released His Faith in Prayer

Faith's Language

The majestic Columbia River no longer flows unimpeded from the Rocky Mountains to the Pacific Ocean. All but 80 feet of the 1,290-foot fall of the river within the United States has been converted into a series of stairs by six federal and five nonfederal dams. These dams were not built to prevent the water from reaching the ocean. They were constructed at a tremendous cost in order to channel the awesome power of this flowing water through special tubes that lead to the water turbines of electrical generators. By directing the energy of the river behind Grand Coulee Dam, the largest and most complex of the dams, the world's largest power plant was created.

Similarly, David's faith was channeled through prayer tubes into divine turbines that generated the power needed to accomplish the job. The existence of reservoirs of faith within David was not sufficient to meet the demands placed on his life. That faith had to be released through channels that would produce energy for the task at hand. Prayer was David's most-used channel. David learned to release his faith when talking to God.

It is sometimes pointed out that Jesus seemed to release His faith by speaking directly to the problem, as when He cursed the fig tree or spoke to the storm on the sea. What may be overlooked is the evidence that Jesus spent long nights of prayer before most of these incidents happened. We should also remember that Jesus said, "I speak what I have seen with My Father" (John 8:38). Jesus said what He had heard His Father say. What had been released as faith to the Father in prayer was later released to the problem as energy.

David did similarly. After his faith had been channeled to Jehovah through prayer, he applied the energy he had released directly to the problem at hand — whether that challenge was Goliath or an entire army. Like us, David had only one faith; but he had a variety of prayer channels through which that faith was directed. David channeled his faith by praying prayers of ...

Petition
Repentance
Affirmation
Yieldedness
Expectation
Rejoicing

Oswald Chambers said,

"Faith by its very nature must be tried, and the real trial of faith is not that we find it difficult to trust God, but that God's character has to be cleared in our own minds .... Faith in the Bible is faith in God against everything that contradicts Him — I will remain true to God's character whatever He may do. 'Though He slay me, yet will I trust Him' — this is the most sublime utterance of faith in the whole of the Bible."[1]

---

1.   *My Utmost for His Highest*, Oswald Chambers, p. 305.

The best way to clear God's character in our minds is to talk to Him. It is also the best way to clear our mental calendar. David learned that if he would weave his day with prayer in the morning, it was less likely to come unraveled during the activities of the day. That is what prayer is all about — communication with Almighty God that calms our frazzled hearts.

David released his faith in prayers of *petition*

David did not try to command mountains to fall into the sea, but he did regularly ask God for divine intervention in his affairs. After one of his miraculous deliverances from the hand of Saul, David sang:

> *I will call upon the LORD, who is worthy to be praised; so shall I be saved from my enemies ... In my distress I called upon the LORD, and cried out to my God; He heard my voice from His temple, and my cry came before Him, even to His ears* (Psalm 18:3,6).

In this instance, David's little band of faithful men were no match for Saul's army, so David did not choose an open confrontation. He hid himself in a cave and cried out earnestly unto the Lord. The rest of the psalm describes how Jehovah miraculously delivered him.

David channeled his faith in a prayer of petition for deliverance, and the power of God was released on his behalf. His faith did not flow out in the open sunlight like a sweeping river, but it filtered down into the dark depths of his despair until it touched the turbine of God's almighty power.

David faithfulness in prayer also touched God to act on his behalf on other occasions:

> *To You I will cry, O LORD my Rock: do not be silent to me, lest, if You are silent to me, I become like those who go down to the pit. Hear the voice of my supplications when I cry to You, when I lift*

*up my hands toward Your holy sanctuary. ...
Blessed be the LORD, because He has heard the
voice of my supplications! The LORD is my
strength and my shield; my heart trusted in Him,
and I am helped; therefore my heart greatly
rejoices, and with my song I will praise Him*
(Psalm 28:1-2,6-7).

This godly king learned the secret of petitioning
God for his needs. Asking in prayer was not beneath
him, nor was it hard on his pride. David was wise
enough to know there were some things he could not
do and faith-filled enough to realize that God can do
everything. Rather than fighting anxiety, David turned
to God for help. Instead of learning to live with the
problem, David prayed. The poet of yesterday's
generation said: "Oh what needless pain we bear. All
because we do not carry, everything to God in prayer."

David unashamedly petitioned God for his needs.
He assumed that nothing was too small or too large for
God. Neither was anything so insignificant that he
could not talk to God about it. Because David saw God
as his Provider and Protector, he boldly made his re-
quests known to Jehovah, never doubting that God
would undertake on his behalf. And God did!

We are encouraged in the New Testament to "...
hold fast the confession of our hope without wavering,
for He who promised is faithful" (Hebrews 10:23), and
to "... ask in faith, with no doubting, for he who doubts
is like a wave of the sea driven and tossed by the wind"
(James 1:6). Like David, we are urged to route our
faith down the prayer tubes to the turbines of God's
great power until what we need becomes a fulfilled
reality in our lives.

David released his faith in prayers of *repentance*

David learned by painful experience what the rest
of us should learn from observation: Guilt prevents

the flow of faith. By virtue of his office, David was able to successfully conceal his sin of adultery — even though it required having Bathsheba's husband murdered. Hiding what he had done, however, did not eliminate the consequences of his actions. The year that followed was one of the most miserable years that David ever experienced. He lost his dwelling place in God's presence, his access to God through prayer and his inner peace. So tormented was he that David admitted: "... my sin is ever before me" (Psalm 51:3). He had hidden the sin from the nation, but he could not hide it from himself or from his God.

Several of David's psalms describe this inner turmoil that occurs when sin is unconfessed and the sinner is uncleansed: "I am poured out like water, and all my bones are out of joint; my heart is like wax; it has melted within me" (Psalm 22:14). "For my life is spent with grief, and my years with sighing; my strength fails because of my iniquity, and my bones waste away" (Psalm 31:10) "When I kept silent, my bones grew old through my groaning all the day long" (Psalm 32:3). What a price for refusing to confess sin!

God mercifully sent the prophet Nathan to let David know that his sin was not hidden from God's view nor blotted out of His remembrance. David made no attempt to justify himself. He had experienced enough separation from the joy of living. He opened his heart and mouth to release his faith in a prayer of repentance that is classic.

Behold, You desire truth in the inward parts, and in the hidden part You will make me to know wisdom. Purge me with hyssop, and I shall be clean; wash me, and I shall be whiter than snow. Make me to hear joy and gladness, that the bones which You have broken may rejoice. Hide Your face from my sins, and blot out all my iniquities. Create in me a clean heart, O God, and renew a steadfast spirit within me. Do not cast me away from Your presence, and do not take Your Holy Spirit from me. Restore to me the joy of Your salvation, and uphold me with Your generous Spirit. Then I will teach transgressors Your ways, and sinners shall be converted to You. Deliver me from bloodguiltiness, O God, the God of my salvation, and my tongue shall sing aloud of Your righteousness. O Lord, open my lips, and my mouth shall show forth Your praise (Psalm 51:6-15).

This prayer is far more than a pleading. It is a proclamation of faith. David was certain that confession would bring cleansing, and that his return to God would bring restoration with God. This certainty may have been in David's heart for the full year he hid his sin, but it did not become effective until he channeled it through the tunnel of prayer to reach the heart of God.

Somewhere the modern Church has picked up the idea that confession of sin is negative. David's prayer reveals that he votes with God that it is positive. His conviction that confession brings wholeness and restoration allowed him to sing: "For I will declare my iniquity; I will be in anguish over my sin" (Psalm 38:18); " ... LORD, be merciful to me; heal my soul, for I have sinned against You" (Psalm 41:4). When David prayed his prayer of repentance, God restored his soul, renewed his health, returned his joy and renewed the Holy Spirit's anointing upon his life. That is a good return on an investment that took him such a brief moment of time. David proved that prayers of repentance are marvelous channels for touching God for forgiveness, restoration and divine favor.

David released his faith in prayers of *affirmation*

A righteous person does not spend all his prayer time confessing his faults. David spent far more time affirming than repenting of sin. He was not satisfied to know inwardly that God was perfect, so he prayed: "As for God, His way is perfect; the word of the LORD is proven; He is a shield to all who trust in Him" (Psalm 18:30). In his melodious affirmation, he strengthened his faith in God and His ways.

David also affirmed God's lovingkindness when he prayed, for he said: "Hear me, O LORD, for Your lovingkindness is good; turn to me according to the multitude of Your tender mercies" (Psalm 69:16). How it helps to pray when God's love and mercy are affirmed along with our afflictions and miseries. David was in the habit of affirming the nature, character and works of God. He called upon God's name (Psalm 8), spoke of God's righteousness (Psalm 36:6), rejoiced in God's judgments (Psalm 103:6), and pleaded God's covenants (Psalm 105:8-11). He steadfastly expected God's victory to be demonstrated in everyday affairs, for he affirmed, "Through God we will do valiantly, for it is He who shall tread down our enemies" (Psalm 108:13).

David's prayers of affirmation were not always concerned with God. Often they were concerned with David himself. He prayed about his integrity:

The LORD rewarded me according to my righteousness; according to the cleanness of my hands He has recompensed me. For I have kept the ways of the LORD, and have not wickedly departed from my God. ... I was also blameless before Him, and I kept myself from my iniquity (Psalm 18:20-21,23).

This was not idle boasting. He challenged the Lord, "Search me, O God, and know my heart; try me, and know my anxieties; and see if there is any wicked way in me, and lead me in the way everlasting" (Psalm 139:23-24). He was open to an adjustment, but he declared in prayer that he felt that his integrity was what God desired. It gave him a positive ground upon which to stand.

David habitually affirmed his faith when he prayed. He said: "In the LORD I put my trust; how can you say to my soul, 'Flee as a bird to your mountain'?" (Psalm 11:1) "Preserve me, O God, for in You I put my trust" (Psalm 16:1). "In You, O LORD, I put my trust; let me never be ashamed; deliver me in Your righteousness" (Psalm 31:1). It must have been valuable to David to affirm his faith in times of prayer, for out of his personal experience of affirming his trust in Jehovah, he exhorts us: "Blessed is that man who makes the LORD his trust, and does not respect the proud, nor such as turn aside to lies" (Psalm 40:4).

David also enjoyed expressing his love for Jehovah when he prayed. His cry was often: "I love the LORD, because He has heard my voice and my supplications" (Psalm 116:1). He also sang, "I will love You, O LORD, my strength" (Psalm 18:1), and exhorted the rest of us: "But let all those rejoice who put their trust in You; let them ever shout for joy, because You defend them; let those also who love Your name be joyful in You" (Psalm 5:11). David realized that love expressed is love amplified. He strengthened himself in his love for God by affirming it vocally when he prayed.

David released his faith in prayers of *yieldedness*

The very act of praying is an adventure in submission. David knew that God expected His people to pray, so he testified: "As for me, I will call upon God, and the LORD shall save me. Evening and morning and at noon I will pray, and cry aloud, and He shall hear my voice" (Psalm 55:16-17). David learned through the years that submitting to prayer and surrendering to the response of God can be two different things. He had watched Saul defy the known will of God to his own destruction, so he purposed in his heart to be a servant who yielded to the will of God.

Prayers that resist God are never productive. David realized that the purpose of prayer is not to manipulate or control Jehovah. Prayer's purpose is to get us into communication with God, so we can know His will and allow it to prevail in our lives. The sooner we yield to this, the more fruitful our praying becomes.

Twice David so yielded to God in prayer that the New Testament writers quote these moments of surrender to Jesus. David's prayer, "Into Your hand I commit my spirit" (Psalm 31:5), is also attributed to Jesus while he was hanging on the cross (Luke 23:46). Additionally, David's words — "I delight to do Your will, O my God, and Your law is within my heart" (Psalm 40:8) — are ascribed to Jesus in Hebrews 10:7. Only yieldedness and surrender of the highest level can result in prayers that are also attributed to Jesus.

In his yieldedness, David opened himself to the perfect will of God for his inner person: "To You, O LORD, I lift up my soul" (Psalm 25:1). Nothing was withheld from his God. Then he pled, "Create in me a clean heart, O God, and renew a steadfast spirit within me" (Psalm 51:10). David desired God's perfect work and will in his soul/spirit. He talked of this to God in prayer.

David's description of his yieldedness to Jehovah is aptly described in his song of degrees. He sang, "Surely I have calmed and quieted my soul, like a weaned child with his mother; like a weaned child is my soul within me" (Psalm 131:2). He walked in confidence and obedience before his God just as he had walked when he lived with his mother.

David quickly yielded to God in the matter of praise and worship. He spoke of lifting his hands in praise, his voice in prayer, his soul in rejoicing and his feet in dancing before the Lord. It is not likely that all this came naturally to David. From his time spent in God's presence, he discovered that God delighted in the praises of His people. Therefore, David praised Him enthusiastically.

David's yieldedness takes on greater meaning when we remind ourselves that David was the most powerful king of his generation. Nations surrendered to his will. Life and death were in his hands, and his word could bring riches or poverty to a person. Yet, David never approached God in pride. He consistently came into God's presence recognizing that He is the absolute, supreme ruler of the earth. In comparison to Jehovah, David said, "But I am a worm, and no man ..." (Psalm 22:6) This, too, is quoted as applying to Christ at His crucifixion. With such a humble and yielded spirit, is it any wonder that David received such great answers to his prayers?

David released his faith in prayers of *expectancy*

Apart from a living trust in Jesus that matures to become an expectancy, prayer is much like putting a note in a bottle and throwing it into the sea. The sender hopes it will reach its destination, but he is not sure it will. David was not a note-in-the-bottle kind of person. He told himself, "My soul, wait silently for God alone, for my expectation is from Him" (Psalm 62:5), and taught others, "Trust in Him at all times, you people; pour out your heart before Him; God is a refuge for us. Selah" (Psalm 62:8).

David prayed with earnest expectation. Thus, he sang: "Lord, I cry out to You; make haste to me! Give ear to my voice when I cry out to You. Let my prayer be set before You as incense, the lifting up of my hands as the evening sacrifice" (Psalm 141:1-2). He expected to be heard; he anticipated an answer. So certain was David that God would hear and respond to His prayers that he confidently declared: " ... the LORD has heard the voice of my weeping. The LORD has heard my supplication; the LORD will receive my prayer" (Psalm 6:8-9). David's confidence in heard and answered prayer is also revealed in this assertion: "But certainly

God has heard me; He has attended to the voice of my prayer" (Psalm 66:19). That is expectation of the highest order.

Because David discovered that God is predictable in His nature, his expectations stretched beyond his anticipation that God would hear and answer his prayers. Thus, he prayed, "Hear me, O LORD, for Your lovingkindness is good; turn to me according to the multitude of Your tender mercies" (Psalm 69:16), and sang, "God has spoken in His holiness: 'I will rejoice; I will divide Shechem and measure out the Valley of Succoth' " (Psalm 108:7). In these seasons of prayer that moved beyond his need to the basic nature and character of God, David learned to rely on the very foundation of God and to expect Jehovah to function consistently in keeping with His essential nature. God never failed David. His responses to David always reflected His character, even as they do today.

David had an expectancy that became a deep, passionate longing for God. When he was in the wilderness of Judah, he cried:

O God, You are my God; early will I seek You; my soul thirsts for You; my flesh longs for You in a dry and thirsty land where there is no water. So I have looked for You in the sanctuary, to see Your power and Your glory (Psalm 63:1-2).

David had been separated from all public worship for a long season as he ran from Saul. This absence from God's tabernacle did not diminish his craving for the presence of God. He yearned for closeness with God and expected to see a manifestation of Jehovah in his lifetime.

A little later in this same wilderness psalm, David cried:

My soul shall be satisfied as with marrow and fatness, and my mouth shall praise You with joyful lips. When I remember You on my bed, I meditate on You in the night watches. Because You have been my help, therefore in the shadow of Your wings I will rejoice. My soul follows close behind You; Your right hand upholds me (Psalm 63:5-8).

His expectancy produced remembrance, rejoicing and response. He remembered God's goodness to him in the past. He rejoiced in the current presence of God in his life — even though he was fleeing for his life — and he responded to that presence by following closely to God's leading.

David released his faith in prayers of *rejoicing*

Like the mighty rushing water of the Columbia River coursing down man-made tunnels to drive the turbines of electrical generators, David's faith was channeled to Heaven's generators through various prayer channels. Whether his prayer was petition, repentance, affirmation, yieldedness, expectation or rejoicing, David let his faith flow when he prayed. God was the primary object of his faith, and David talked to God when he prayed.

Perhaps David's favorite prayer channel was *rejoicing*. He wrote a song for the chief musician that ended: "But I have trusted in Your mercy; my heart shall rejoice in Your salvation. I will sing to the LORD, because He has dealt bountifully with me" (Psalm 13:5-6). In one of his meditative songs, David testified: "I have set the LORD always before me; because He is at my right hand I shall not be moved. Therefore my heart is glad, and my glory rejoices; my flesh also will rest in hope" (Psalm 16:8-9). Speaking as the leader of the nation, David promised, "We will rejoice in your salvation, and in the name of our God we will set up our banners! May the LORD fulfill all your petitions" (Psalm 20:5), and instructed his constituents:

Rejoice in the LORD, O you righteous! For praise from the upright is beautiful. Praise the LORD

*with the harp; make melody to Him with an in-
strument of ten strings. Sing to Him a new song;
play skillfully with a shout of joy* (Psalm 33:1-3).

David's concept of rejoicing was melodious and active. He wasn't content with mental attitudes. He
wanted them expressed. David rejoiced openly and enthusiastically when he was dealing with his God. He
also loved to have the rejoicing released in concert
with others. Therefore, he exhorted:

*Let them shout for joy and be glad, who favor my
righteous cause; and let them say continually,
"Let the LORD be magnified, who has pleasure in
the prosperity of His servant"* (Psalm 35:27).

In David's mind, the rejoicing had its origins in God
Himself. Hence he declared:

*He has put a new song in my mouth — praise to
our God; many will see it and fear, and will trust
in the LORD* (Psalm 40:3).

*Let all those who seek You rejoice and be glad in
You; let such as love Your salvation say continually, "The LORD be magnified!"* (Psalms
40:16 and 70:4)

*I will extol You, my God, O King; and I will bless
Your name forever and ever. Every day I will
bless You, and I will praise Your name forever
and ever. Great is the LORD, and greatly to be
praised; and His greatness is unsearchable. One
generation shall praise Your works to another,
and shall declare Your mighty acts. I will
meditate on the glorious splendor of Your majesty, and on Your wondrous works* (Psalm 145:1-5).

David's language of faith was a prayer language
released to Jehovah, who was the object of that faith.

Once he had talked to God, David found himself far more capable of directing his faith to the problem at hand.

Chapter 6

David Transformed His Life With Faith

Faith's Alteration

When I pastored a thriving congregation in a community through which the Columbia River flowed, the area was a barren, desert land. I used to join the men of my congregation in hunting rabbits in the sagebrush and desert plants. We joked about the worthlessness of the territory. We could have purchased an acre of that land for less than five dollars, but what good would it have been?

Then, in 1952, the first water from the reservoir behind the Grand Coulee Dam on the Columbia River was released for the Columbia Basin Irrigation Project, the largest single irrigation project in the Northwest. As this water became available for the destitute land, a transformation took place. The land proved to be very fertile, and productive farms now replace the fields where I once hunted rabbits. Today this land sells for thousands of dollars per acre — and I could have purchased it for almost nothing!

What changed the value of this land? The availability and application of life-giving water to the

arid land. The river that once flowed only in the gorge
was made available to the land through giant pumps
and hundreds of miles of irrigation ditches. Without
the water from the river, the land had been useless for
centuries. Likewise, the river, without the land, had
never produced a crop. When, however, the river and
the land came together, there was an abundance of
productivity. This is a classic example of the New Testament teaching that "faith without works is dead"
(James 2:20).

David was a man of the soil. Although he special-
ized in sheep, he was aware that a season of drought
destroyed the pasture land. During such seasons he
sought regions that had a water supply in order to
have grass for his flock. David was also mindful of the
spiritual parallel to the physical reality. Thus, he
wrote: "O God, You are my God; early will I seek You;
my soul thirsts for You; my flesh longs for You in a dry
and thirsty land where there is no water" (Psalm 63:1).
He knew that without a touch of God in his life, he
would wither and die.

Although he experienced these seasons of dryness,
David firmly believed that it was God's will that this
king live and be spiritually productive. The psalm that
follows reflects that belief: "You visit the earth and
water it, You greatly enrich it; the river of God is full of
water; You provide their grain, for so You have
prepared it" (Psalm 65:9). Just as God regularly visited
the earth with rain, so He consistently filled David's
heart with life-giving faith. In one of the psalms that
was written to be sung in public worship, David wrote:
"He shall send from heaven and save me; He
reproaches the one who would swallow me up. Selah.
God shall send forth His mercy and His truth" (Psalm
57:3). These faith-producing graces that God rained
down on David transformed arid areas of his life just
as irrigation water transformed the desert into rich
farm land.

David's faith transformed his worship

David knew how quickly worship dries up and is worthless without a liberal application of faith. He wrote: "Offer the sacrifices of righteousness, and put your trust in the LORD" (Psalm 4:5). The worship of his day centered around the sacrifices at the Brazen Altar, but David observed that it was often little more than empty ritual. While the penitent brought the sacrifice, the priest performed the ritual on his or her behalf. Most of the worship was by observation rather than participation. Often the Israelite felt quite distant from the God he sought to worship.

David called for a return to heartfelt zeal and trust when worshipers brought their sacrifices to Jehovah. He testified, "But as for me, I will come into Your house in the multitude of Your mercy; in fear of You I will worship toward Your holy temple" (Psalm 5:7), and implored his people, "Oh come, let us worship and bow down; let us kneel before the LORD our Maker" (Psalm 95:6).

Although the New Testament had not yet been written, David knew from experience that worship without faith is not pleasing to God: "Without faith it is impossible to please Him, for he who comes to God must believe that He is, and that He is a rewarder of those who diligently seek Him" (Hebrews 11:6). No amount of sacrificial offerings could make up for a lack of faith and trust when worshiping the Almighty God.

The Lord Jesus Christ completely fulfilled all the typical meanings of the sacrifices of the Old Testament. He was the end of substitutionary sacrifices, but the performance of rituals still replaces the offering of heartfelt worship. The Sunday morning bulletin distributed in many churches suggests that worship is singing hymns, praying prayers, participating in responsive readings, giving offerings and listening to sermons. This is no more worship than slaying sheep and goats. These acts may be channels for or tools of worship, but in themselves, they are not worship. Without living faith flowing in those activities, they are but religious rituals that are putrid in the nostrils of God and powerless in the lives of believers.

David could not conceive of worship without the presence of God. Even when fleeing from King Saul, David had a priest with him. Some of his greatest psalms of worship were written during this season of his life, indicating that he never lost his faith in God. Instead, David directed that faith into the worship of God and drew strength, comfort and guidance from it.

After he was crowned king of the combined kingdoms, David initiated the return of the Ark of the Covenant to Jerusalem. There he erected David's Tabernacle to house this symbol of Jehovah's presence to serve as a center for worship. David assembled musicians, singers and priests to minister here before the Lord twenty-four hours each day. David's faith to worship was demonstrated in his actions. He prepared to worship, he provided for worship, and he participated in worship. This attitude toward worship is evidenced in the following words: "Give unto the LORD the glory due to His name; worship the LORD in the beauty of holiness" (Psalm 29:2). David allowed the faith God had placed within him to transform his worship from mere form to an active relationship with Jehovah.

David's faith transformed his love

David discovered by trial and error that, fundamentally, worship is love responding to love. God's self-revelation is a demonstration of His love. That love for us has been called grace. When we channel that love to others it is affection, but when we return God's love for us back to Him, it becomes worship. The First Epistle of John proclaims: "In this is love, not that we loved God, but that He loved us and sent His Son to be the propitiation for our sins. ... We love Him because He first loved us" (1 John 4:10,19). Receiving this revelation of God's love for us demands an action of faith. God said it, but our faith must seize it.

David realized that doubt in the Lord's goodness and wisdom when he was in the midst of problems and distress would soon make his heart cold toward God. He learned, however, that if in those same circumstances his faith strengthened its hold upon God and His promises, love burst forth into full blossom. We, too, have learned that faith and love will increase or diminish together every time.

The apostle Paul said, "Now may the Lord direct your hearts into the love of God ..." (2 Thessalonians 3:5), but David may have originated the concept. David challenged his people, "Oh, love the LORD, all you His saints! For the LORD preserves the faithful, and fully repays the proud person" (Psalm 31:23).

Faith expresses itself through love, so love flourishes exactly as faith flourishes. Paul taught us, "For in Christ Jesus neither circumcision nor uncircumcision avails anything, but faith working through love" (Galatians 5:6). Paul was convinced that faith must flow through the channel of love. He consistently wrote of this inner connection of faith and love, as evidenced in this reminder to the Ephesians: "Peace to the brethren, and *love with faith*, from God the Father and the Lord Jesus Christ" (Ephesians 6:23).

David proved that faith works by love. Love reacts upon faith and adds to its power, for love forbids unbelief. The wife who deeply loves her husband has great faith in his abilities, capacities and character. When this trust is violated, her love begins to diminish and it needs the bolstering of renewed faith. So it is in our walk of faith. Love just will not let us doubt. When the mind declares defeat and failure, love asserts its healing balm and encourages the will to hold on a little longer. Faith and love are the great allied principles of the Christian life. As Dr. Perkins wrote, "Faith is the cause of love, and love is the fruit of faith."

A Puritan once wrote, "Faith and love are the two arms and the two eyes without which Christ can neither be seen nor embraced." We dare not play one against the other or seek to develop one more than the other. We need both of these oars if we are to row our boats to the other side. But some people mistakenly believe that one or the other virtue is sufficient. They should not be surprised, then, when all their motion results in turning circles. No amount of faith can compensate for a lack of love, nor can an abundance of love indemnify a lack of faith. But faith's presence can transform weak love into strong love.

David's faith balanced his love

It is interesting to note that David connects his initial faith experience with his mother's breasts. He sang: "But You are He who took me out of the womb; You made me trust when I was on my mother's breasts" (Psalm 22:9). Many years later his son Solomon wrote the love poem we call the Song of Solomon, in which he twice describes the beauty of his bride's breasts, emphasizing their beautiful symmetry. He even refers to them as twin deer that feed among the lilies (Song of Solomon 4:5). Much later, Paul exhorted believers to "stand therefore, having girded your waist with truth, having put on the breastplate of righteousness" (Ephesians 6:14). In reference to this, I wrote in my book *Let Us See Jesus*:

> "For the purpose of provision, nourishment, comfort and strength, the Bride of Christ is to be well-developed, just as that of a mature woman in the natural. Some churches are very strong on faith, but they don't have much love; others have a great deal of love, but they don't have enough faith to handle the church budget. Both

extremes are badly out of balance; neither has the perfect symmetry of a beautiful, fully developed woman. God wants His church to have equal development in the areas of faith and love.

"When it is noted that God is developing faith or love in His church, some say, 'Isn't it wonderful that God is finally calling out His church?' No — He's had His church all along, but now He's emphasizing the need of full development in these areas. God allows a group to go just so far in the faith realm; then He does not allow further development until His dealings begin to produce a flow of love. Or, conversely, in the people who flow so well in love, but not so much in faith, He cuts off the love and deals in the development of faith, so there will not be a lopsided presentation of His kingdom; for God is a God of balance.

"When we are strong in faith and weak in love, faith does not have a proper channel to work through. This is probably why we see some very awkward things produced by men of faith who have not love. Some are always calling for 'equal time' to preach their ideas, but God is calling for 'equal development' for adequate presentation of His Gospel."

David knew that faith and love are partners who lose their distinct individualities. He realized that the saints may love Christ until they have poured out all their spikenard upon Him and have washed His feet with tears and until they have totally exhausted the fountains of the deep within themselves, but this will not substitute for faith. If faith were present, these actions of love would be a channel for faith's release; but they cannot become the creative cause for faith.

David's faith transformed his unbelief

David had a sure foundation for his faith — God's Word. This godly king wrote: "As for God, His way is perfect; the word of the LORD is proven; He is a shield to all who trust in Him" (Psalm 18:30). David knew that his only defense and shield against unbelief was implicit trust in God and His word. Consequently, his spirit easily joined the expression of another psalmist who sang, "Your word I have hidden in my heart, that I might not sin against You" (Psalm 119:11).

David was not without his times of fear, but experience taught him that fear had to be handled as quickly as possible, for the longer he waited, the stronger it got. Fear of the enemy can quickly become unbelief in the protection of God. Likewise, fear of failure easily becomes unbelief in God's presence and power, and fear of present problems borders on unbelief in God's provision and promises.

David knew that either he must conquer his fear, or his fear would soon consume him. If he gave way to cowardice, he forever forfeited courage. If he lived in dread, he was soon filled with doubt and unbelief. This is a lifestyle no Christian can afford to maintain.

David's life and reign reveal his conviction that unbelief is the mother sin; from it issue all others. All the iniquities for which men and women manifest a propensity stem from this fundamental sin of unbelief — the unwillingness to let the faith that God has imparted and inspired be released back to God — for where unbelief is preeminent, evil will predominate. As the New Testament later affirmed, "Beware, brethren, lest there be in any of you an evil heart of unbelief in departing from the living God" (Hebrews 3:12).

During his wilderness wanderings, David learned that unbelief is not the opposite of faith; it is the absence of faith. (Fear is faith's opposite.) Where unbelief prevails, faith's efficacy is stifled and faith's operation is opposed. David wrote: "Teach me Your way, O LORD; I will walk in Your truth; unite my heart to fear Your name" (Psalm 86:11).

David understood that faith — or *trust*, as he called it — is fundamental to the spiritual realm. It is the bottom line, the prime ingredient and the unparalleled force in Christian living. It is the absolute, irreducible minimum without which we continue to be locked up in our tiny time-space dimension, totally unaware of a timeless and limitless God who is beyond our contact. David dared not let unbelief replace his faith. All God's promises to him were dependent upon that faith.

As a shepherd lad, David saw enough evidence of Jehovah to trust Him. He wrote:

The heavens declare the glory of God; and the firmament shows His handiwork. Day unto day utters speech, and night unto night reveals knowledge. There is no speech nor language where their voice is not heard (Psalm 19:1-3).

David was consistently convinced that people are not without evidence for faith in God; they willfully function in unbelief in spite of the manifest proofs around them. They choose not to believe the evidences presented daily, nor will they accept the testimony of those who have been participants in God's goodness.

David never ceased to be amazed that, whether through fear, wonder or rebellion, the carnal nature of people grasps unbelief as though it were a life line to a sinking swimmer, when, in fact, it is a confirmed one-way ticket to hell. Jesus substantiated David's conviction when He declared, "Therefore I said to you that you will die in your sins; for if you do not believe that I am He, you will die in your sins" (John 8:24). David knew that no person is doomed for lack of faith, but rather for an unwillingness to exercise that faith toward Christ.

David deliberately channeled his faith and trust onto the barren ground of unbelief and transformed it back into faith. He refused to be so agitated with his fears and doubts that he wouldn't appropriate the faith that had previously been stored in his life. Instead, he responded out of the abundant supply of trust that had developed out of his relationship with God and His Word and turned his unbelief into productive faith.

David's faith transformed his doubts

The word *doubt* is not used in any of David's psalms, but he was repeatedly confronted with its power. *Doubt*, as the word is used in the New Testament, is "a wavering, a hesitancy or a staggering in faith." It is not unbelief itself, but more a poor handling of unbelief. Doubt is somewhat like trying to tune in a weak radio station; it wavers in and out, usually getting less and less discernible until it fades completely. Hiding in the caves or in the woods of the wilderness, there were times when David's faith signals were very weak.

Experience has shown that when we begin to withdraw from God's Word, to discriminate between what we will read and what we will not read, and to hesitate in believing what God is saying, we are already involved in doubt. Doubt is uncertainty about God's promises. Doubt lacks confidence in the God of these promises and considers their fulfillment very unlikely. Doubt puts our experience against God's Word and trusts in our reasoning more than in reality. David discerned that doubt is the first tool satan uses against the human race: "Has God indeed said ...?" (Genesis 3:1)

David was never in danger of drawing back into apostasy, but that is not what doubt is anyway. Doubt is simply hesitating, reexamining or questioning what has already been proven. It is not honest inquiry; it is a wavering in faith after faith has come. As such, doubt is one of the greatest enemies of faith, for it dissipates faith after faith has been received.

David learned that one of the fatal characteristics of doubt is its presumption that what we see, hear, feel and taste in this world is real, and what God speaks of in His spiritual kingdom is unreal. He simply accepted the truth that if God says it is real, not only is it real, but by faith, he could reach into God's realm and make it become a living reality in his world of sense and space.

David watched doubt at work in the lives of his companions. He discovered that doubt is always costly, but particularly so when it becomes a dominant force in a moment of crisis. David learned something of the high price Jacob paid in doubting the word of God's angel, when he needlessly gave a fortune in cattle to his uncle Laban. He saw firsthand something of the cost Abraham and Sarah paid for acting in doubt and bringing Ishmael into the world. He also closely observed the tremendous price King Saul paid for doubting God in a moment of pressure. From these experiences, David determined that he would not doubt.

David learned that when God speaks, faith flows and we generally believe and obey. But during the action of obedience, our minds begin to rationalize the situation, often producing doubts of such magnitude as to totally short-circuit our faith and make it of no effect. The old cliché is well worth remembering: "Never doubt in the darkness what you trusted in the light." The time for double-checking is when God is speaking. Once we get into the battle, it is too late to try to determine what God has said. Having put our hands to the plow, it is far too late to look back. If obedience is an act of faith, doubt will stop faith's action and soon produce disobedience. The resulting penalty will be severe.

David refused to resurvey a problem once God had spoken. He refused to speak his fears afresh or introspectively search his heart for the resources necessary to produce victory, for he knew this would become a breeding ground for doubt. Instead, David took decisive action against the entrance of doubt into his mind, knowing that the longer doubt remained with him, the more difficult his struggle to displace it would be. David irrigated the doubting area of his life with the life-giving water of faith.

David's faith transformed his presumption

David was blessed with true faith or trust. Such divine faith does not presume! Faith is a settled persuasion, not a pretense or a presumption. God's faith comes as a result of a directed word from Him, and it flows into the persuasion that "God has said ..." Faith will not go beyond God's word because it stakes its life on that word.

Presumption, on the other hand, lacks a word from the Lord. It assumes that because a promise is written in the Bible, it is available to anyone who chooses to act upon it. Interestingly enough, however, none but Naaman has ever been cleansed from leprosy by dipping seven times in the Jordan River (see 2 Kings 5), nor have I ever read of anyone but Peter walking on the Sea of Galilee with Jesus (see Matthew 14). These were direct words from God to specific individuals that became faith-producing words. Trying to force God to repeat these miracles by stubbornly stepping over the stern of a ship or by dauntlessly dipping seven times in the Jordan River would not be faith; it would be preposterous presumption. In either case, one would get wet, but that is all.

Using the wisdom with which God had endowed him, David prayed, "Keep back Your servant also from presumptuous sins; let them not have dominion over me. Then I shall be blameless, and I shall be innocent of great transgression" (Psalm 19:13). David knew that as surely as no husband has the right to "presume" he knows what his wife is thinking, and no wife is entitled to "presume" she knows her husband's desires and will, so we have no right to "presume" God's desire to do, say or act in a specific way.

David knew the living God, so he didn't need to presume upon Him; he could ask Him. He sensed that since God is a person, he shouldn't violate Him. We with David must learn that Jehovah is Almighty God; we dare not dethrone Him. To do so is to be perilously presumptive, and God not only hates presumption but He classifies it as a dangerous sin that, under the old covenant, deserved death.

Every time the word *presumptuous* is used in the Bible, it refers to a bad character trait that is contrary to the life of a believer who has learned to walk in the Spirit. The presumptuous person is revealed to be insolent, proud, arrogant and elated or lifted up. He speaks whether God has spoken or not. He acts irrespective of the commands of God and predetermines his actions in spite of those commands. The apostle Peter says that presumptuous ones "despise authority" and are so self-willed that "... they are not afraid to speak evil of dignitaries" (2 Peter 2:10). They even claim that God has spoken to them when, in fact, God did not speak to them at all.

David was king over all Israel. He dared not act presumptuously, for his actions affected the entire nation. This king continued to allow God to be sovereign and did not seek to impose his will upon the Almighty. David never sought to originate faith by mental attitudes and emotional responses, and he refused to declare that the product of these inner forces — that at its highest level is natural or human faith — is divine faith. He recognized faith as a gift from God and never tried to produce what only God can initiate.

David knew that unless God speaks, nothing will happen, for mountain-moving faith must originate in Almighty God, not in presumptuous little men. David never viewed himself as a creator, nor did he yield to the arrogance that tries to take God's place. He was always happy to let Jehovah be the Creator because he recognized the sin of presumptuousness.

When David was tempted to act unilaterally because of a pressing need, he deliberately paused to let his faith flow into this barren field of presumption. Then he was always delighted to see the transformation that took place. Whether he was resting comfortably in God's Word or waiting until God spoke to the situation, David always sought and cherished the word of the Lord.

Chapter 7

David Developed His Faith

Faith's Enlargement

The Columbia River flows 1,214 miles from its source, Columbia Lake in British Columbia, to the Pacific Ocean at Astoria, Oregon. Although evaporation, absorption and irrigation districts deplete the amount of water that flows down this great river, there is a continual increase in the water volume because the Columbia drains some 258,000 square miles of territory. Seven major rivers flow into it during its long course to the Pacific Ocean. In addition to these, the ocean tides flow 140 miles upriver. In spite of the vast amount of water taken out of the river by man-made projects, the river continues to get larger the further it flows.

This is very much like David's faith. The longer he lived and the more he used his faith, the stronger and larger it became because David learned the secret that enabled him to have more faith at the end of his journey than at its beginning. While faith is a gift from God, it can be enlarged and developed through usage and by the addition of other scriptural qualities.

David's faith was sterling

It is easy to forget that David had access to the books of Moses and the historical books up through

Joshua. He was aware of God's dealings with Israel in her early years as a nation. No nation on the face of the earth has ever been more aware of the direct intervention of God in her national affairs than Israel. Delivered from slavery and directed to the Red Sea where God could decontaminate them from their former captors once and for all, Israel became a nation under God in a day. David knew that God had faithfully defended His people, defined His laws, demonstrated His power, and devoted Himself to supplying every physical and spiritual need of His people. Jehovah designed a tabernacle for a meeting place between Himself and His people, deputized Aaron as their priest and commissioned the entire tribe of Levi to assist the people in their worship. Israel was declared to be the people of Jehovah, and they submitted to complete dependence upon Him in everything.

David's psalms prove that he knew Israel lacked nothing from the day she left Egypt to the day she entered Canaan — nothing, that is, except faith. For Deuteronomy 32:20 tells us that the Lord said: "I will hide My face from them, I will see what their end will be, for they are a perverse generation, *children in whom is no faith.*"

David understood that Israel did not lack provision; she lacked the performance of faith. The parting of the sea, the sweetening of Marah's waters, the daily manna, the guiding cloud, the smitten rock that provided continuous water — plus the voice of God — all were faith producing. They were incontestable evidence of God's goodness, grace and glory. Yet Israel did not trust the Lord. Her unfaithfulness was revealed in murmuring ten or more times, in seeking to return to Egypt's slavery several times, in making a golden calf as a replacement for God, and in secretly carrying images of Egyptian gods throughout all her wanderings.

In spite of her frowardness (perversity, disobedience), fear and idolatry, Israel never admitted
her lack of faith. Instead, she faked it. Tabernacle services never ceased, sacrifices were never discontinued,
feast days were faithfully observed, and the cloud was
dutifully followed all the days of the wilderness
wanderings. The people still performed as though they
had faith, but they were hypocritically pretending. We
might call Israel's faith "stainless steel." Outwardly it
looked fine and it was utilitarian, but it lacked intrinsic worth.

In contrast to this, David's faith was sterling. It was
pure silver in the sight of God. It was divine in nature
and it carried the stamp of God's approval. David was
unusual in that he seemed to learn from history.
During his wanderings in his own personal wilderness
while fleeing from King Saul, David maintained his
trust in Jehovah. He never provoked God with idols,
nor did he murmur against God's provision or leadership. David loved with a pure love, walked in true
obedience, and believed God with total abandon. His
worship was consistent and continuous. His conviction that God would bring him to the throne never les-
sened in spite of the many obstacles that hindered his
ascension to this high office. David's faith did not
come from a Moses who had met God. David had met
God personally, and the faith that flowed from
Jehovah to David remained steadfast and sterling to
his dying day.

David's faith was sent

Since faith is altogether a supernatural thing, there
is no way that mixing our natural faith with it can enlarge, expand, augment, extend or increase it in any
way. Jesus told Nicodemus, "That which is born of the
flesh is flesh, and that which is born of the Spirit is
spirit" (John 3:6), to which someone added: "and never
the twain shall meet." We recognize that no amount of

culture, education or affluence can elevate natural life into eternal life. Similarly, we accept that our natural love can never mature into divine love, for the Scriptures clearly state, "In this is love, not that we loved God, but that He loved us and sent His Son to be the propitiation for our sins" (1 John 4:10), showing that agape love flows from God to man, not the reverse. In the same way, divine faith comes only from the Almighty God and cannot be increased by our human concepts or emotions. This is why David never spoke of enlarging his faith or trust. He knew that he was incapable of producing or increasing true faith. The faith he possessed had been sent to his heart by God for the purpose of energizing his life.

David either knew instinctively or he learned by experience that faith, divine faith, is not a spiritual muscle that enlarges with exercise. Neither is it an intellect that expands by study and speech. Faith is a divine gift, a spiritual fruit and a wholly supernatural, divine energy. Yet it is measurable, for Paul declares that "... God has dealt to each one a measure of faith" (Romans 12:3), and that measure is increasable: "And the apostles said to the Lord, 'Increase our faith' " (Luke 17:5). Though it is measureable, true trust and faith is not reproducible; it is only receivable.

God is both the source and the object of our faith. We need not produce or attempt to reproduce faith, for there is an abundance of faith in God beyond the capacity of any person or groups of people to exhaust it. God never intended that we should learn how to *develop* faith. He merely wants us to learn to *use* it. David learned this lesson very well.

David's faith was *not* a seed

It is probably fortunate that David was never exposed to the modern teaching of "seed faith," for David never thought of the faith God had imparted into him as a seed that would grow and develop into something greater. Although Jesus did tell His disciples that faith the size of a grain of mustard seed could move mountains (see Matthew 17:20), His emphasis was on the minute quantity of faith required to do great exploits, not on the living ability of a seed to grow and enlarge itself.

Only once in the entire Bible do we read of faith growing, and that is in Paul's introductory remarks in his second letter to the church in Thessalonica, in which he says, "We are bound to thank God always for you, brethren, as it is fitting, because your faith grows exceedingly, and the love of every one of you all abounds toward each other" (2 Thessalonians 1:3). The Greek word we have translated "grows" is *huperauxano*, which means "to increase above ordinary degree." This is the only time in the entire Bible where it has been translated "grows." When true growth process is signified, such as the mustard seed's phenomenal growth, the Greek word employed is *anabaino*, which means "to arise, ascend, climb, come up, or grow." If Paul had thanked God that the Thessalonian saints had successfully nurtured their faith until it had grown from a seed into a tree, he would have used *anabaino*; but he deliberately chose the word *huperauxano*, which signifies an abundant increase without meaning that the faith had produced the increase. It was not the inherent nature of faith that caused it to increase; these saints had learned the secret of returning repeatedly to the source of faith in order to receive an ever enlarging supply of divine energy.

David learned in his walk with Jehovah that faith is not enlarged by planting a seed of faith and watching it grow, but that "... faith comes by hearing, and hearing by the word of God" (Romans 10:17). Faith is not a plant in God's garden; it is an energy inherent in His nature. David knew that he could not plant, cultivate, nurture or reproduce faith any more than he could raise a harvest of divine holiness, omnipotence or mercy.

In one of the psalms that David wrote for public worship sessions, entitled "To the Chief Musician," he wrote,

> *Here is the man who did not make God his strength, but trusted in the abundance of his riches, and strengthened himself in his wickedness. But I am like a green olive tree in the house of God; I trust in the mercy of God forever and ever* (Psalm 52:7-8).

These verses reveal that David understood the difference between trying to produce a basis for faith and coming to God to receive that faith. As a tree in the house of God, David continually drew on Heaven's resources of divine faith and love.

In his book, *The Real Faith*, Dr. Charles Price (under whom I was privileged to study in my younger days) says,

> "One of the chief difficulties is our failure to see that faith can be received *only* as it is imparted to the heart by God Himself. Either you have faith, or you do not. You cannot manufacture it ... you cannot work it up. You can believe a promise, and at the same time not have the faith to appropriate it. ... No matter how much you nurture and cultivate the spirit which the world interprets as 'faith,' it will never grow into *faith* which was introduced by Jesus in the days of long ago."

David's faith could swell or surge

The Columbia River lacks the capacity to reproduce itself. Loss of water as it flows should diminish it to a small stream, but the seven major tributaries that run into it enlarge it far beyond its original flow.

Similarly, David's faith was only receivable, not reproducible. Yet, through the addition of other Christian virtues, his faith was rounded out and given broader expression in his daily behavior. This is equally true for us. We cannot cause faith to reproduce itself, but we can add complimentary ingredients that increase the measure and value of our faith.

Simon Peter addresses his second epistle to those who share the faith he has received from God: "Simon Peter, a servant and apostle of Jesus Christ, to those who have obtained like precious faith with us by the righteousness of our God and Savior Jesus Christ" (2 Peter 1:1). After reminding his readers that grace and peace come through a knowledge of Jesus Christ, he continues:

> But also for this very reason, giving all diligence, **add to your faith virtue**, to virtue **knowledge**, to knowledge **self-control**, to self-control **perseverance**, to perseverance **godliness**, to godliness **brotherly kindness**, and to brotherly kindness **love**. For if these things are yours and abound, you will be neither barren nor unfruitful in the knowledge of our Lord Jesus Christ (2 Peter 1:5-8).

God has given us seven tributaries to flow into our stream of faith. As in cooking, the seven Christian graces can be added to, blended into, and harmonized with the divine faith that has been obtained from God, but they do not increase that measure of faith. They merely flavor it, give it texture and color, and become its fragrant aroma. They are not so much the bread crumbs in the meat loaf of faith as they are the salt, pepper and spices.

Furthermore, none of these seven Christian excellences can ever substitute for faith, for while they are attracted to faith as steel is attracted to a magnet, they no more possess the energy of faith than nails possess the energy of a magnet. While faith may flow through all of these additions, lending its energy to and through them, they never become faith itself — only the channels of faith.

In addition to these seven areas of goodness that should gravitate to the pure divine faith we have received from God, there are other fruits of righteousness that grow on the branches of our lives, very much as individual grapes mature into a cluster. These interact together with faith to the extent that it becomes very difficult to think of one without the other. Usually these correlatives of faith are complementary, oftentimes they are supportive, and sometimes they are expressions of God's faith in our lives.

Who can completely separate faith and love? It is for certain that David could not. He wrote: "But let all those rejoice who put their trust in You; let them ever shout for joy ... let those also who love Your name be joyful in You" (Psalm 5:11). Thus, he connects trust, joy and love. Love is the very channel through which faith works! How can faith and hope be divided when hope is often the fountainhead out of which faith flows? Similarly, when trust is taken out of faith, or when faith seeks to operate without obedience, we have an anemic, forceless faith that may have been divine in its origins, but has been greatly weakened in its operation in our lives.

We generally find it difficult to discuss faith without speaking of believing, or to explain faith's operation without referring to the fruit and gift of faith, for these are so integrated with our understanding of faith as to almost make these words synonymous terms in our vocabularies. But, as David knew, none of these realities, experiences or actions is faith. Each is a subsidiary of faith, a portion of the parcel, a correlative of faith, but faith stands above and beyond all them put together. Each flows into the faith channel increasing the volume, enhancing the flow of divine energy, and giving its special flavor to the faith received from God.

David's faith was strengthened

The seven tributaries Peter says should be allowed to contribute to our faith not only give character and flavor to our faith, but they strengthen that faith. David became a mighty warrior, a statesman, a leader of men, and a king not only because he possessed the faith of God, but because he added Christian virtues to that faith to strengthen it and increase its value.

David certainly added virtue to his faith. As we have already seen, he did not hesitate to speak of his integrity and righteousness when speaking to God. His behavior demonstrated the depth of his faith. By our standards, David did many things we would question. By the standards of his day, he lived a very virtuous life.

David continually added knowledge to that virtue. His knowledge of God never ceases to amaze me. In my first book on David, *David Worshiped A Living God*, I point out that he knew the nature of God better than many of the prophets. David was never satisfied with the promises of God. He consistently sought to know the One who made the promises, and he succeeded beyond most men of his generation. His faith was undergirded and strengthened through his knowledge of God.

David knew that faith in God's person will always involve faith in God's promises, for God and His word are inseparable. Faith is the force that not only enables us to believe the veracity of God's promises but also helps us to grasp them and to bring them into fulfillment in our lives. To know the Word and to believe that it is actually the Word of God does not change either our conditions or our circumstances. We, like David, need to mix faith with the promises to effect the desired result. The more we know God and His Word, the stronger our faith will become.

David showed himself to be a man of self-control. When Saul came into the cave where David was hiding, the men with David urged him to kill Saul right there. But David was able to control his emotions. Similarly, when David came into Saul's camp and found Saul asleep, his armorbearer pled with David for the right to thrust Saul's spear into his heart, but David would not touch God's anointed. This self-control strengthened David's faith.

David's moral perseverance, godliness, brotherly kindness and love are found in his psalms like the fragrance of perfume. Each added strength to the faith that David had received. The New Testament strongly declares that the spiritual character of the individual in which faith flows adds to the working of that faith. James insisted: "The effective, fervent prayer of a righteous man avails much" (James 5:16). God hears the prayers of all persons, but prayer that rises from the heart of a godly person seems to have a priority status in Heaven. David was a godly man whose moral virtues added strength to his faith. He perceived that virtue empowers strength, for he wrote: "Cast your burden on the LORD, and He shall sustain you; He shall never permit the righteous to be moved" (Psalm 55:22).

David's faith was simple

No one who has studied the life of David would ever call him simple. He was a complex individual who was talented in many areas and capable beyond most men of his age. But while he was quite complex, his faith remained very simple.

In years gone by, Harold Horton used to declare the following in his conferences both in England and America:

"Faith is difficult only in its absolute simplicity. Faith is not grasping tight and clenching fists and furrowing brows and gritting teeth and shouting in a kind of hopeless hope, 'I will believe; I do believe.' No; that is not faith. Faith is the easy, restful, fearless attitude of an infant reposing on its mother's breast — with no thought of fear, effort, or uncertainty. Faith is absolute rest in God, absolutely knowing and absolutely trusting according to His gracious promises and commands."

The simplicity of faith has become a stumbling block to our complex society that has become accustomed to computers, color televisions and space exploration. Since we have so few simple things left in our lives, we tend to relegate faith to the same category as a walk down a country lane or homemade ice cream. We generally see faith as something in our pasts that has been superseded by an improved product. The factual nature of this attitude is revealed in the words of Matthew Henry:

"True faith is an old grace, and has the best plea of antiquity: it is not a new invention, a modern fancy. The eldest and best men that ever were in the world were believers. They were an honor to their faith, and their faith was an honor to them. It put them upon doing the things that were of good report."[1]

It is not truthful to say that faith has been superseded by an improved product in our generation. While faith in God has steadily been replaced by faith in science and faith in humanity, only the blind and the biased would call it an improvement. Let the record speak for itself. Compare our society of 50

1.   *Commentary on the Bible*, Matthew Henry and Thomas Scott, Vol. 3.

years ago with its present condition and see what replacing faith in God with humanism has done to us.

David maintained a simplicity in his faith. Whether he was facing Goliath or dealing with angry King Saul, David's faith remained in Jehovah. Even after the kingdom was secured to him, and peace, for the most part, reigned in his expanded kingdom, David retained his simple faith in the Almighty God who had so faithfully brought David this far. His desire, in his aging years, to build a temple for God shows that David still had faith in the dynamic presence of a living God.

While David could not enlarge his faith, he did continue to grow in God's faith. He never found it imperative to replace that faith, nor was he ever embarrassed to be dependent upon God's faith. he seemed to feel that what God had begun, He would complete, and if God started by imparting faith, He would continue to impart and respond to that faith. Thus, David grew in faith continually until his dying day, never losing his desire to strengthen that which God had given to him. That is also God's will for each of us.

Too often as we mature as Christians, we lose the simple faith that brought us to Christ. Our lives may be complex, and certainly God is complex beyond the capacity of the greatest theologians to fully understand Him, but His faith must remain simple. Its source is in Himself. He simply asks that we receive it and release it — it is not important that we understand it.

David remained content to be a channel for this divine energy without seeking to analyze, dissect or comprehend it. That is one reason why his faith remained so consistent throughout his lifetime.

Chapter 8

David Undergirded His Faith

Faith's Foundation

An abundance of water is not necessarily a river. It may form a lake or flood fertile valleys. A channel and a riverbed are the necessary ingredients that cause the vast waters of the Northwest to form the Columbia River. For most of its long course to the ocean, the Columbia River is channeled into deep gorges where it is efficiently undergirded by a riverbed of solid rock or of large boulders. When the Lord spoke through Isaiah to promise, "For I will pour water on him who is thirsty, and floods on the dry ground" (Isaiah 44:3), He seemed to imply that the condition of the land would determine the results. Those areas that were prepared (thirsty) would benefit, but the same water would be destructive to the unprepared (dry) ground.

Just as water without a riverbed can become a destructive flood, so faith without a proper undergirding — without preparation for its flow — can be wasted, at best, and destructive, at the worst. David prepared a riverbed in his life through which divine faith could flow.

David prepared the channel — not the faith

It is not redundant to again state that while men and women are not inactive in the production of faith, they are not the initiators of it. Faith does not have its origins in the hearts of people, but in the word of God. Faith is a heavenly grace made available by God's mercy through His word.

As I stated earlier, Harold Horton said "Faith is the normal atmosphere of Heaven." Certainly, then, it would be an abnormal atmosphere on earth, for sin has so defiled the place of our residence that it no more resembles God's homeland than darkness resembles light. For one to live on earth in the atmosphere of Heaven would require a transfusion, transference or transmission of God's atmosphere into man's atmosphere. Although it cannot be synthesized or produced by man any more than darkness can produce light, it, like light, can be beamed into the darkness, transforming it into brilliant brightness. The more light, the greater the brilliance.

David did not attempt to produce his faith any more than the Columbia River tries to create its source, the St. Lawrence Lake. In my book *Let Us See Jesus*, I wrote:

"Faith is produced by God, not by man. Faith is a divine energy, not a religious one. It has its origin in the Godhead, not in the Body of Christ. We're not capable of producing this dynamic of faith, only of receiving it. In the same manner that homeowners don't produce electricity — they only consume it — so we do not produce faith — we only utilize it. Furthermore, the generator that produces electricity does not consume it; it transmits it. Similarly, God does not produce faith to consume it, but to transmit it. We receive faith not to learn how to produce it, but to learn how to release it.

"Faith's source is God the Father, God the Son, and God the Holy Spirit, not in the Bible, not in theology, not in doctrine, although sometimes doctrine is called 'the faith.' The Bible, theology and doctrine will direct faith, but will not produce it.

"Faith is not even produced by prayer, fasting or works, though these might release faith. Fasting for faith might produce a weight loss, and working for faith may bring about exhaustion, but faith is not produced by man's efforts; its source is totally in God: 'God has dealt to every man the measure of faith' (Romans 12:3)."

David undergirded his faith with God's Word

Although David lived long before the New Testament was written, he learned that divine energy flows from God's words. He wrote: "I will worship toward Your holy temple, and praise Your name for Your lovingkindness and Your truth; for You have magnified Your word above all Your name" (Psalm 138:2). David equated God's name with His divine nature, but he learned that Jehovah had chosen, for our sake, to place what He has said to us above the revelation of His intrinsic nature.

After this revelation David wrote: "In the day when I cried out, You answered me, and made me bold with strength in my soul" (Psalm 138:3). He learned that divine energy, which is faith, flows when God speaks. Paul declared the same thing when he wrote: "So then faith comes by hearing, and hearing by the word of God" (Romans 10:17). While God is talking — at the very moment when he speaks — faith is transmitted via the voice channel of God. Divine energy accompanies God's voice, and the Bible calls that energy *faith.*

Obviously, then, it is not sufficient to merely know the Bible intellectually, or to have its records stored in the memory circuits of the mind. Many people can say perfectly the catechism of their church, but they are faithless in their approach to both God and life. Knowledge often gets locked into the brain without affecting the heart. True faith touches the heart, since faith is emotional as well as intellectual.

God's Living Word, Jesus Christ; God's written Word, the Bible; and God's preached Word are all intended to produce, inspire and direct faith. It is not the dead letter of the written word, however, nor the historical account nor even the rhetoric or the oratory of the preachers that produces this divine faith. It is the Living Word, which emanates from the presence of God Himself, that changes our atmosphere into His atmosphere. It is God's Word on the wings of His Spirit through whatever channel He may choose that illuminates our darkness, dispels our doubts, and infuses us with His faith.

This action, however, is not one-sided. Those people who desire faith are required to be participants in this change from a natural to a spiritual atmosphere and from an absence of faith to a fullness of faith. Paul declares that *hearing* is an essential condition for the reception of faith. No amount of divine speaking will be effective unless there is a genuine hearing of the word spoken. First, of course, there must be an availability of the speaking. For the most part, this is not a problem in our world. There are few, if any, places left on our planet where God's word is not proclaimed. Although some of us give the message in massive doses, while others seem to give it with an eyedropper, Bible translations, radio and television transmissions, Christian travelers, and missionary teachers have reached nearly all nations. The critical component is not how often or how much the message has been proclaimed, but in what measure it has really been heard.

To have a useful flow of faith, then, we need both to create a channel of God's word in our lives and to develop a listening ear. David did this from his youth to his old age. He studied what written Scriptures were available to him, and he spent time listening to the Living Word of God speaking to him in times of prayer and fellowship. David undergirded his faith with communication from God.

David undergirded his faith by communicating with God

David knew that faith cannot generate in man's heart, but he learned that it can degenerate rapidly. Faith is less like the permanent magnet and far more like the electric magnet that must be energized every time it is used. Somehow our beings do not store up faith on a continuous basis; we need to be energized and reenergized by the power of the Word. Like muscular energy, faith can be exhausted and must be replenished.

God freely provides faith, but we must appropriate it. Unfortunately, we often work so hard trying to produce it that we fail to simply procure it. Although it is available without a price tag, an expenditure of great energy, or a demonstration of great righteousness, we often fail to meet God's requirement that we listen to what He is saying to us through His Word. God has provided faith for every man. It's our job to give our attention to what He supplies.

While faith is nonproducible and easily procurable, it is also expendable. That is, when faith is exerted and applied, it becomes exhausted — used up — and must be replaced. This is why Jesus spent nights in prayer after major ministries. He was charging His spiritual batteries. If the Son of God was aware when virtue (power) had gone out of Him (see Mark 5:30), then the rest of us would do well to replenish our faith levels.

Looking at the life of David convinces me that David regularly renewed his faith through communication with God. Many of his psalms are prayers to God in which he pours out his fear, anger and frustration and waits to hear what Jehovah replys. Psalm 59 is a classic example of this avenue of communication between David and God.

David wrote this psalm when Saul, seeking a chance to kill him, sent men to watch his house. He begins, "Deliver me from my enemies, O my God; defend me from those who rise up against me," (Psalm 59:1) and then asks God to "consume them in wrath, consume them, that they may not be; and let them know that God rules in Jacob to the ends of the earth. Selah" (Psalm 59:13). In praying this prayer of vengeance, David must have touched God, for he ends the psalm singing:

> *But I will sing of Your power; yes, I will sing aloud of Your mercy in the morning; for You have been my defense and refuge in the day of my trouble. To You, O my Strength, I will sing praises; for God is my defense, the God of my mercy* (Psalm 59:16-17).

David moved from seeking reprisal to songs of rejoicing. What was the turning point? He touched God in this communication, and faith began to flow anew.

David knew that as soon as he heard God speak, there would be a rekindling of faith and trust. How often these psalms flow from exasperation to excitement. In trying to apprise God of the situation he was facing, the king often got a new glimpse of the sovereignty and mercy of God. David frequently moved rather abruptly from pronouncing curses upon his enemies to declaring his praise for Jehovah. When he touched the fountainhead of faith, his fears abated, his courage rose, and his doubts vanished. David then turned from rebuking the enemy to praising God.

God still renews and strengthens His people through prayer. When we communicate with God our faith is renewed until the enemy and his works seem unimportant compared to the glory of God we have touched. We, too, will turn from rebuking satan to rejoicing in the Lord when our faith is strengthened in the divine presence.

Whenever we recognize that our faith is ultimately in God, not ourselves, we cease introspective searchings for the faith to meet a crisis and rest silently in the security of the presence of Christ. Like the child whose fear of the dark disappears the moment Daddy sits on the edge of the bed, the awareness of the Lord enables us to commit our anxieties and fears into His loving care. He is our faith; He is perfect faith. Intimate fellowship with Him is our best assurance of continuing faith.

Both biblical and secular history reveal that men of great faith have also been men of intimate relationship with the Lord. The entire patriarchal story is presented to exhibit the lives of the servants of God who lived by faith. It was their implicit self-commitment to God that set them apart from other men. When we come to the New Testament, we find their lifestyles called lives of faith. In the Old Testament, they were described as men who walked with God. These men of faith talked with God, reasoned with Him, covenanted with Him, and dared to obey Him. Their faith was not a self-energizing force; it was a by-product of a living alliance with the God of all faith.

David undergirded his faith by believing

What is called *obedience* in the Old Testament, becomes *believing* in the New Testament. It is the divinely accepted response to the quickened Word of God when God communicates with an individual. David may not have used the word *believe*, but he was quick to obey God.

When God speaks, something always happens. All creation was spoken into existence by God. "God said, 'let there be ...' and there was ..." (Genesis 1:3) Nothing can remain the same after God speaks to it.

> *For the word of God is living and powerful, and sharper than any two-edged sword, piercing even to the division of soul and spirit, and of joints and marrow, and is a discerner of the thoughts and intents of the heart* (Hebrews 4:12).

The energy of God's Word is a cause that demands an effect. The Bible calls that reaction, or effect, *believing*.

Faith and *believing* are so integrally connected that it is difficult to think of them separately. Yet, it is desirable to do so since the New Testament makes a consistent distinction between them by the context that surrounds them. The foremost contrast between these words is that faith has its source in God, while believing has its origins in persons. Faith, as a divine commitment, requires believing as a human confession of God's committal.

Faith is a force received; believing is that force released. Perhaps it would be fair to say that faith is God's attitude shared with persons, while believing is the action of those persons based on that attitude. Faith is an assurance, and believing is our assent to it. Faith is an affirmation; belief is an admission. Faith is the confidence; believing is the credence. Faith is a trust; believing is obedience. Faith is a God-given ordinance; believing is our observance of that ordinance.

If faith is a reliance, then believing would be a response. If faith is a persuasion, then believing must be the performance. If faith is a cause, then surely believing would be its effect. It would be doctrinally and practically accurate to say that faith is the *eye* of the soul, which looks out toward God's promises and represents them clearly and convincingly to us, while believing is the *hand* of the soul, which lays hold of the contents of those promises and applies them to human behavior.

Faith's purpose is to produce performance. It expects to be coupled with believing because it is fruitless until it is so united. We hear and then heed, we see and subsequently respond, until our inner knowing is translated to an outer act of believing. Believing is the only acceptable response to faith that is taught in the New Testament.

After His death and resurrection, Jesus' disciple, Thomas, openly refused to believe the testimony of the remaining ten disciples to Christ's resurrection. Eight days later, Jesus appeared to all eleven disciples at one time. "Then He said to Thomas, 'Reach your finger here, and look at My hands; and reach your hand here, and put it into My side. Do not be unbelieving, but believing' " (John 20:27). The process Jesus used to bring Thomas from faithlessness to faith was not merely a change in his mental attitude. It involved the physical activity of seeing and touching. The faith Christ's presence produced was released in believing action — one supported the other. It was not, however, until action released his faith that Thomas was turned from "doubting Thomas" into "believing Thomas."

David had the same experience, as do we. Truth, no matter how reinforced it may be, does not vitally affect our lives until we act on that truth in a believing demonstration of obedience, a joyful response of praise, or an active participation in the promise. Indeed, believing gives action to our faith, undergirding it and releasing it to flow in its proper channel.

Because David learned that faith has its source in God and is channeled through the communication of His Word, he strove to develop a more intimate relationship with God that expanded his measure of faith, not his intellectual concepts or emotional responses. When faith increases, believing also increases.

Faith and believing are as inseparable as incense and fragrance. They are coupled together like love and marriage or clouds and rain. It is the first, faith, that induces the second, believing. When they are properly blended, a third quotient is also produced. Incense and fragrance produce an emotional sensation; love and marriage create a family; clouds and rain yield productivity on the earth; and faith and believing bring spiritual realities into our natural world.

That David learned to immediately respond to imparted faith with the action of believing is shown when he sang, "When You said, 'Seek My face,' my heart said to You, 'Your face, LORD, I will seek' " (Psalm 27:8). David believed that God meant what He said, and he responded with believing action. This was a bedrock undergirding to the flow of his faith.

David undergirded his active faith with passive faith

It is likely that David understood the difference between passive faith and active faith better than we do because He was surrounded with evidences of passive faith. The heart of the worship of his generation was obedience to the law, which codified the promises God had given to Israel and directed that nation to proper responses of faith. Inasmuch as the ultimate promise of the law and the prophets was that of a coming Messiah, the law gave direction to their lives until the Messiah came; for, as Paul points out, "Therefore the law was our tutor to bring us to Christ, that we might be justified by faith" (Galatians 3:24). The communication of promise to the patriarchs was faith in the active sense, while the codified promises in the law were a passive form of faith.

In the New Testament, this passive form of faith is generally preceded by the definite article, i.e. *the* faith.

Following the early events in the brand-new Church, the Book of Acts records, "And the word of God spread, and the number of the disciples multiplied greatly in Jerusalem, and a great many of the priests were obedient to the faith" (Acts 6:7). Already the experience of the Day of Pentecost, with the subsequent teaching of the apostles, was sufficiently codified to be called *the faith*, and a great company of the priests were willing to step out of the old system into the new.

The faith in the New Testament is the systematic declaration of the promises of God and the doctrines that grow out of the embraced promises given to us by God. It is a set of propositions or a religious creed or an article of belief that germinates out of an intimate association with God and His Word. It is no more a replacement for faith than the law was a replacement for promise. *The faith* becomes a foundation, a support, an undergirding for our faith. It is also a guide, a compass and a checkpoint for our faith. It is our safety in hearing from God, for every communication of a *rhema* is subject to what has already been declared in the *logos*.

David embraced *the* faith. He was a lover of the codified law of God and a student of what had been written. Whether he realized it or not, he was, in his psalms, enlarging the passive faith of Israel. His actions prove that this was not a substitute for active faith, but an undergirding of the flow of faith that came from the presence of Almighty God.

None of the writers who were used of the Holy Spirit to define, describe or delineate faith intended to replace subjective faith with objective faith. Rather, they were like Jude, who wrote,

> *Beloved, while I was very diligent to write to you concerning our common salvation, I found it necessary to write to you exhorting you to contend earnestly for the faith which was once for all delivered to the saints* (Jude 1:3).

Similarly, the apostle Paul urged the saints at Philippi to "... stand fast in one spirit, with one mind striving together for the faith of the gospel" (Philippians 1:27).

David realized that since our concept of God will greatly affect the level and attitude of our faith, it is important that we regularly read, seriously study, and constantly contemplate the doctrines of God's Word, for none of us will live long enough to learn the full life of faith on a trial and error basis. Rather, "... all these things happened to them as examples, and they were written for our admonition, on whom the ends of the ages have come" (1 Corinthians 10:11). The successes and failures of a life of faith are faithfully recorded in the Scriptures as object lessons for those who yearn to learn to live by faith. The instruction and teaching on faith shared by the New Testament writers was given to enable others to embrace the principles of faith in Jesus Christ and the subsequent blessings and benefits a life of faith can bring to the believing saint.

The life of David illustrates that whenever we mistake *the* faith for God's faith, we are doomed to failure and subsequent confusion in trying to exercise that faith. *The* faith is passive; God's faith is active. *The* faith defines, while God's faith does. *The* faith affects attitude; God's faith begets action. Each needs the other, but neither can substitute for the other. We cannot live without the teaching of the Word, but we also cannot function without the flow of divine faith. We need both the passive and the active aspects of faith in our lives, and we need to know the difference between the two. Peter would never have succeeded in walking on water if he had tried to function on a written promise from the prophets. His success was undergirded by a living word from Christ Jesus Himself. Ideally, then, we will be both Bible students and intimate friends with Christ, for the highest level of faith flows out of an in depth relationship with Jesus Christ.

David was completely willing to let God produce and provide the faith. He was equally eager to undergird that faith so it could flow with minimum hindrances through all the dry places in his life in order to bring a spirit of refreshing, renewing and rejoicing to his being. David's worship was vibrant because his faith was so completely undergirded that nothing could prevent its flow in praise, adoration and worship to Jehovah.

Chapter 9

David Revitalized
His Faith in Praise

Faith's Attitude

Since the Columbia River drains 85 percent of the watershed of the entire northwestern United States, during the rainy season it is often very muddy. As tons of top soil and silt join the Columbia from one of its seven major tributaries, it looks almost solid enough to walk across. This sediment sinks into the riverbed as the river flows downstream and the mighty Columbia begins to cleanse and purify itself. The river is clear and attractive again after a few miles.

Faith's flow tends to do this for our lives. The storms of life consistently fill us with silt and filth. It is difficult to tell a Christian from an unbeliever at times, but as the river of faith flows in the spirit of the believer, it begins a process of cleansing and purification until once again the beauty of holiness can be seen. Faith in the finished work of Christ at Calvary revitalizes our lives and cleanses us from the contamination of the world. As the apostle John put it, "But if we walk in the light as He is in the light, we have fellowship with one another, and the blood of

Jesus Christ His Son cleanses us from all sin" (1 John 1:7).

David learned this lesson. He experienced the defilement inherent to living. He sometimes reacted very unrighteously in pressure situations, but he released a flow of faith in his spirit that kept him in a living relationship with Jehovah that brought him back to pristine purity again and again.

Although this cleansing is seen repeatedly in David's life, the early stages of his flight from Saul are classic examples. Jealousy caused King Saul to react in anger toward David. Repeatedly he attempted to kill this young contender to the throne until it became so dangerous for David to remain in the palace that even his close friend, Jonathan, Saul's son, urged David to flee for his life.

David went to his home only to have soldiers come to arrest him. Michal, his wife, convinced them that he was ill in bed and sent them away. Then she slipped David out a window and put clothing in his bed to make it look like David was asleep. When King Saul discovered this, his anger knew no bounds and he immediately began a search for David.

Stopping by the priestly city of Nob, David secured some shewbread for food and took for his weapon the sword of Goliath, which had been kept as a trophy of war by the priests. He then fled to the Philistine city of Gath, where he pleaded for sanctuary. King Achish was open to this request, but "the servants of Achish said to him, 'Is this not David the king of the land? Did they not sing of him to one another in dances, saying: "Saul has slain his thousands, and David his ten thousands" ?' " (1 Samuel 21:11) This produced a level of fear in David such as he had never experienced before. He stood as a single individual surrounded by Gathites who were stunned to see him carrying the sword of their former champion, Goliath. David realized too late the foolishness of parading a victory over an enemy in front of his former comrades.

Quite obviously, David was quick-witted. We read,

Now David took these words to heart, and was very much afraid of Achish the king of Gath. So he changed his behavior before them, feigned madness in their hands, scratched on the doors of the gate, and let his saliva fall down on his beard (1 Samuel 21:12-13).

It worked. King Achish questioned David's sanity in appearing before him in the first place, but after seeing David's actions,

Achish said to his servants, "Look, you see the man is insane. Why have you brought him to me? Have I need of madmen, that you have brought this fellow to play the madman in my presence? Shall this fellow come into my house?" (1 Samuel 21:14-15)

David's praise refocused his attention

It was a close call for David, but he escaped. Hastily he recrossed the frontier and entered Saul's kingdom, but his life was still in great jeopardy. To return to the court was impossible, and he dared not risk involving his relatives by seeking shelter at Bethlehem. His only apparent alternative was to adopt the life of a fugitive and wander in the hills of Judah, which were familiar to him because of his years of shepherding there.

Two miles up the valley of Elah from Gath is a labyrinth of hills and valleys that is deeply honey-combed with caves. One of these, near the ancient Canaanitish city of Adullam, offered David the shelter he needed. Called the cave of Adullam, it is described as a dark vault with a small window-like opening in the perpendicular face of a cliff. Here, on the border between Israel and her enemies, David hid from Saul,

...and everyone who was in distress, everyone who was in debt, and everyone who was discontented gathered to him. So he became captain

over them. And there were about four hundred men with him (1 Samuel 22:2).

This Adullam cave experience was a muddy time for David. He had deceived Saul by pretending to be sick, he had taken and eaten the sacred shewbread, and he had fled for his life. (While in the cave, he learned that all the priests of Nob had been slain by Saul for aiding his escape.) He had also been deceitful to King Achish. Now his family, plus the 400 people who were also fleeing from Saul, had joined him. David's defiled conscience and the weight of the cloudy responsibility that had been thrust on his shoulders made him a different person. He didn't act like the lad who had tended his father's sheep or the young man who had slain Goliath. Nor was he the same David who had played and sang before King Saul to dispel demonic influences. Life had drained its silt and mud into David's life so that his beauty was compromised and his duty was cloudy.

The arrival of his parents presented a peculiar problem because David was convinced that they could not survive, at their age, the rugged life of fugitives. Thus, David risked his life and went to Moab to plead with the king for asylum for his parents. After it had been granted, David retraced his steps, convinced his parents that they would be safer and more comfortable in Moab, and then secreted them out of Judah in complete privacy. Because his parents were in jeopardy because of him, David was forced to activate faith in God's protection and provision while filling his responsibility as a son. Although he was the youngest son, he felt responsible for them. It was his faith in action that got them through to safety.

Who understands the lines of communication that develop in times of danger? King Saul couldn't find David, but mysteriously the news of David's retreat to the shelter of the cave spread swiftly throughout the whole land. Those who were severely pressed by misery, poverty and bitterness of soul began to flock around him. This anointed, but uncrowned, king soon found himself the leader of 400 men — all rebels. Their only common denominator was their hatred for Saul. While anger can be a mighty motivating force, it is difficult to control — especially when there is no one or nothing upon which that anger can be vented.

Although David had successfully led divisions of Saul's army, they had been trained, disciplined soldiers. Now David had to exert a strong faith in God to develop the untrained, unskilled revolutionaries who had come to him into a fighting unit with survival skills. What had begun as simple faith for personal survival expanded to faith for the well-being of his parents, his brothers and 400 desperate men. David had the anointing for leadership, but now he was developing the necessary skills for leadership. As he learned that a true leader focuses his attention away from himself onto those he is leading, the weight of this responsibility caused David to cry: "Lead me, O LORD, in Your righteousness because of my enemies; make Your way straight before my face" (Psalm 5:8). Knowing his limitations, David extended his faith to God's unlimited ability to preserve and protect him. This king-in-training felt secure in his leadership only as God led him. David did not place his faith in his personal abilities. His faith was in God's leadership. What a lesson for each of us. "Follow me as I follow Christ" must be our motto.

David's praise released his anxieties

It is not easy to hide and provide for 400 fugitives. The long hours of inactivity must have heightened the discontent and frustration of these men. Amidst all the disgruntled talk and expressions of anger by these fugitives, David began to sing: "I will bless the LORD at all times; His praise shall continually be in my mouth" (Psalm 34:1). Simple logic suggests that David should have sung of his victory over Goliath as he polished that fallen warrior's sword, but David elected to be involved in the present rather than the past. He realized that former victories would not get him through his present circumstances. Samuel's cry at Ebenezer — "Thus far the LORD has helped us" (1 Samuel 7:12) — may have been comforting, but it offered little release from present collective apprehensions.

The anxiety in the hearts of these men was nothing compared to the heightening anxiety in David. He had more than a prevailing peril with which to contend. He had a divine promise blazing in his heart of sitting on the throne, yet he was in a dark cave with a motley crew of discarded humanity around him. David lacked even the slightest hint how to get from the cave to the crown.

Unable to solve his personal problems, David let his faith redirect his attention to Jehovah. Thus, he sang in front of his men, "My soul shall make its boast in the LORD; the humble shall hear of it and be glad" (Psalm 34:2). In the dark hole of hiding, David boasted in the Lord.

Faith enables us to ignore present circumstances while embracing future promises. David may have been sitting on a protruding boulder on the floor of a cave, but his faith was sitting on the throne in the palace. His spirit rejoiced in the God who not only made promises but performed what He pledged.

David learned that the most valuable release of anxieties comes in the midst of praising the Lord. This did not immediately change his circumstances, but it did change his inner attitudes. David, who had to be prepared to fight at a moment's notice, dared not live with a continual inner fight. He had to pour out those anxieties in order to lead his men comfortably. His faith easily praised the Lord and boasted in the goodness of Almighty God, for he knew that God was unchangeable. The mercy David had known in the past would preserve him in the present.

David's praise reunited him in fellowship

David's time in the cave isolated him from the activities of the palace. During his years in the palace he had led men into battle and had busily engaged himself in the affairs of state that Saul had entrusted to him. Now he had to use the skills of passive waiting he had learned as a shepherd. He was prepared to wait for God's time. Although he was pursued by Saul, he never retaliated. As he waited to come into leadership in God's way, this perpetual refrain characterized his songs: "My soul, wait silently for God alone, for my expectation is from Him" (Psalm 62:5). David sat in patient submission until God made his foes the footstool of his feet and set him as His king on His holy hill of Zion.

As righteous as all this appears to us, it was lonely for David. Separated from his wife, home, friends and family, David had to make a new life for himself. His limited resources made this difficult — especially when his only associates were totally dependent upon him.

In the midst of this, David cried: "Oh, magnify the LORD with me, and let us exalt His name together" (Psalm 34:3). His first desire was to be reunited in fellowship with the Lord. He chose to magnify the Lord instead of his problems. Refusing to blame the Lord for all that was happening to him, David preferred to bless the Lord for His person. Although God had not yet elevated him to His chosen throne, David reached for the fellowship of being in God's heart.

After praise refocuses our attention and releases our anxieties, it has a way of reuniting us in fellowship with God. It brings our attention to His glorious person and reminds us of His past provisions. Praise lifts us from our thoughts of gloom to His throne of grace. It also erases our loneliness as we begin to espouse

His loveliness, for exalting God excites an awareness of His nearness.

David handled much of his loneliness through praise, but this cry was not singular. David also appealed to his companions to share in his worship and praise of Jehovah. He knew very well how important it was to have a rallying point for his men. Thus, "let us exalt His name together" was his cry. He was not yet free to lead his men into battle, but he found it safe and sensible to have them gather with him in sessions of praise to the Lord. These moments created a unity of purpose and action within these men and allowed them to join David in an expression of worship.

As a pastor, I found congregational praise to be a powerful, uniting force. On repeated occasions when tensions seemed to be dividing the congregation, I would lead them in earnest praise of the Lord. Finding a commonality in this action seemed to diffuse the pressure of differences that had arisen among us. Being able to do something together stirred the family spirit anew.

David capitalized on this. In Psalm 34, written in the cave of Adullam, he appeals to his men three times to join him in praise. In verse three, he asks them to magnify the Lord with him and exalt His name unitedly. In verse eight, he exhorts: "Oh, taste and see that the LORD is good; blessed is the man who trusts in Him!" (Psalm 34:8) Then in verse nine he adds: "Oh, fear the LORD, you His saints! There is no want to those who fear Him" (Psalm 34:9). David wanted to fellowship with his men in four stages:

(1) In magnifying the Lord

(2) In exalting the name of the Lord

(3) In experientially tasting the goodness of the Lord

(4) In living in the fear (reverence) of the Lord

David preferred this level of fellowship over the fellowship of a common enemy, a common hatred or a common fear. So should we!

David's praise rebutted the enemy

We see Saul as David's enemy, but David consistently refused to accept this concept. He knew that Saul was driven by jealousy, envy and demonic spirits. When these were absent, Saul was David's friend. So David refused to see Saul as an enemy when these were present. David realized that *fear* was his major enemy. Saul could not function beyond the will of God, but David's inward fear could prevent the will of God from being fulfilled in his life. David wisely attacked his true enemy. He needed to discredit his fears. This was essential both for himself and for the sake of the fearful men he led, because a fearful man who leads fearful people is dangerous to everyone around him.

In the psalm of the cave, David addressed his fears. First he said, "I sought the LORD, and He heard me, and delivered me from all my fears" (Psalm 34:4). David didn't want to discipline himself to accept his fears, he wanted deliverance from them. He trusted God for that deliverance. Every time he left the cave, he had to handle his fears. Every time another person came to him in the cave, he felt fear, for if this person could find him, how long would it be before Saul located him?

One of the great powers of faith is its consistent deliverance from fear. Either trust or fear will dominate our lives, but somehow the two cannot coexist. David sang, "Whenever I am afraid, I will trust in You" (Psalm 56:3).

Trust (faith) was David's answer to fear. David believed that "the angel of the LORD encamps all around those who fear Him, and delivers them" (Psalm

34:7), so he could testify, "I lay down and slept; I awoke, for the LORD sustained me" (Psalm 3:5).

David learned that his faith could deliver him from his fears, but he also learned that faith can direct our fear from an enemy to God. He cried: "Oh, fear the LORD, you His saints! There is no want to those who fear Him" (Psalm 34:9). The fear David speaks of here is reverential awe, which is worship. Rather than waste emotional energy trying to deal with his fears, whether real or imagined, David let God's presence deliver him from his terror. Then he turned what had been negative energy into the positive energy of praise and worship.

By turning to the Lord to deal with his enemy, David completely discredited and invalidated the enemy. He more than pulled its fangs; he cut off its head. Instead of fighting his fear of discovery, David flaunted his delight in the Lord in the face of his fears. His godly fear of the Lord overrode his natural fear of self-preservation. As a worshiper, he was fearless. As a warrior, he was stimulated by fear. Molding this motley crew into a fighting unit was fear inducing, but leading them into praising the Lord was fear relieving. For this reason, David said, "Come, you children, listen to me; I will teach you the fear of the LORD" (Psalm 34:11). He wanted them to follow his example and learn to negate the power of fear that gripped their lives. He needed confident men, not cowards. Often the difference between the two is merely how fear is handled. David wanted it to be handled through worship.

David's praise retuned his spirit

Every musician knows the necessity of tuning and retuning his or her instrument. Even the finest of instruments gets out of tune when it is played. David sensed that his faith was like that. Sometimes it got out of tune and needed an adjustment.

Sitting in the darkness of the cave in the stillness of the night, David had repeated opportunities to replay in his memory those places where his faith was obviously off pitch. Separated from other worshipers, he wondered if it would have been better if he had stayed with the prophets. He most likely regretted to his dying day that he had stopped by the priestly city of Nob to get food and a weapon, for his request for aid had caused the death of all but one of them. Couldn't he have trusted God for provision then, even as he was being forced to trust God for provision now? Hadn't that sword of Goliath's been more of a detriment to him than a blessing? And what about that incident in Gath? Does a man of faith have to pretend to be crazy?

There had been many sour notes since David had fled from Saul. True, he had not lost his faith; but it was getting badly out of tune. This musician determined to take time to tune his instrument before playing any more concerts.

Convinced of his need for revitalized and redirected faith, David began to boast in the Lord. Because he had discovered that the Lord is the perfect pitch to which all other instruments are tuned, David rejoiced: "I sought the LORD, and He heard me ..." (Psalm 34:4) Once he picked up the correct pitch, David began the necessary adjustments. He knew that the tongue is the first string to go flat, so he told himself, "Keep your tongue from evil, and your lips from speaking guile" (Psalm 34:13). David wanted his mouth to be in tune with God's words.

Once he had tuned his speech, David tuned his actions: "Depart from evil, and do good ..." (Psalm 34:14) Faith is far more than correct words; it is shown in correct deeds. David had not only spoken faithlessly, he had done some things that were very out of tune with God's true faith.

The next string David sought to bring to correct pitch was his attitudes. "Seek peace, and pursue it," he commanded his soul (Psalm 34:14). He certainly needed this string to be in tune with God, for he was in a constantly threatening situation where he was surrounded by men who wanted to release their anger and frustration in a good fight. While Paul told Timothy: "Fight the good fight of faith, lay hold on eternal life, to which you were also called and have confessed the good confession in the presence of many witnesses" (1 Timothy 6:12), that fight of faith is usually in our own minds, where we need to maintain the faith God has given us, and in our spirits, where we must remain at peace.

The fourth string David tuned was the string that reverberated in the presence of Jehovah. Without that divine presence, the other strings would be like "sounding brass or a clanging cymbal" (1 Corinthians 13:1). In the midst of his distress, David cried: "The LORD is near to those who have a broken heart, and saves such as have a contrite spirit" (Psalm 34:18). David brought himself to an awareness of God's nearness in the depth of the cave of Adullam. If, in that cave, with so many things to distract him and the constant presence of his men, David was able to realize the presence of God, how much more possible it must be for us!

David retuned his faith instrument, for there were many concerts to be played on it before he reached the throne of Israel. Musician that he was, David knew the value of tuning the instrument before playing the concert.

David's praise revitalized his faith

Every pianist knows that a freshly tuned piano almost reaches out, demanding to be played. Similarly, properly tuned faith is a revitalized faith. In this psalm, David sang: "Come, you children, listen to me; I will teach you the fear of the LORD" (Psalm 34:11). His fear of the Lord was vibrant.

David knew that godly fear is the beginning of an affiliation with God out of which true faith can flow. This fear-inspired relationship is absolutely essential, both for obtaining and maintaining living faith. We must see Him, serve Him, fear Him and love Him before we can be enabled by Him. Faith is not a faucet to be turned on and off at man's will; it is a flow of the very nature of God Himself that comes out of an intimate relationship with God.

This fear of the Lord — this divine awe — is God's answer to man's anxiety, uneasy conscience and divided loyalties. When we properly submit to the fear of the Lord, our anxieties about ourselves and our world are transformed, leaving us with this fear alone, which is a trembling adoration of the transcendent Holy Lord. Too frequently, however, this noble form of fear degenerates as the true nature of God is less and less clearly understood. Then it becomes a paralyzing sense of terror. Instead of fearing God, as we are commanded, we fear ourselves, our circumstances, our future and our declared spiritual enemy, the devil.

This deteriorated form of faith is graphically displayed by the disciples when the evening storm almost swamped the boat in which Jesus was soundly sleeping. Fearfully awakening Him and charging Him with unconcern over their plight, they were astounded at His authority as He calmed the wind and the waves. Thus, they exclaimed one to another, "Who can this be, that even the winds and the sea obey Him?" (Matthew 8:27) If they had but known who He was, the disciples would have taken a nap with Him instead of submitting their hearts to terror. Terrorizing fear in the life of the believer is always the result of a lack of the true "fear of the Lord." Our weak, limited knowledge of His nature causes us to think that circumstances are out of His control and perhaps that the devil has some almightiness after all.

Whenever we turn our attention from knowing God in our endeavors to living a life of faith, we open ourselves to this immobilizing force called fear. Faster than we would have believed possible, we discover that this fear has stopped sound thinking, exaggerated our difficulties, murmured at Christian duties, and even blamed God for the bitterness of soul and spirit that remain as a residue of faith.

David so revitalized his faith through praise that he ended his song with: "The LORD redeems the soul of His servants, and none of those who trust in Him shall be condemned" (Psalm 34:22). What confidence! What trust! What living faith! Especially when we remember it came from the lips of a man who had just recently redeemed his own life by playing insane.

Chapter 10

David Activated His Faith

Faith's Obedience

The Columbia River has many obstacles to impede its flow — huge boulders, narrow canyons, debris fed by the tributaries and, more recently, man-made dams. At times, it seems that the river will cease to flow and form a massive lake, but the pull of gravity upon the water causes it to find a way through, under or over the impeding barriers.

Faith, too, is often impeded in the lives of believers. Natural fears, mental doubts, satanic interference and human opposition can slow the flow of our faith to a trickle. At these times, people are tempted to deny having any faith, but the faith God imparted is not destroyed. It is merely dammed up so that it cannot flow.

David experienced this. Some of the psalms he wrote during the years he wandered in the wilderness show that his faith was blocked by something. His faith flow was barely discernible. It seemed that God had forgotten His timetable as years had passed with little or no change. During those years, as Saul got closer and closer to killing him, David wondered if he would ever gain the throne. Psalms 10, 13, 17, 22, 25,

44 and 69 are all credited to this season of his life. Each of them expresses a fit of mistrust that shows David's faith was obstructed. Listen to him cry: "How long, O LORD? Will You forget me forever? How long will You hide Your face from me?" (Psalm 13:1) "Save me, O God! For the waters have come up to my neck. I sink in deep mire, where there is no standing; I have come into deep waters, where the floods overflow me" (Psalm 69:1-2). Fortunately, David recognized the danger signs of a diminished flow of faith and began exercises that would release the restrictions and restore the volume of faith he had once possessed.

David activated his faith through love

There are some things in this life that, in spite of their dissimilarities, are almost always thought of together, as though one without the other would be incomplete. For instance, we traditionally couple bread and butter, potatoes and gravy, men and women, and love and marriage. Interestingly enough, God's Word couples *faith* and *love* more than a dozen times in the New Testament. Although they are different qualities, they are dependent upon each other. Faith in Christ is the mainspring of action, which is regulated by the law of love. Or, to put it another way, faith makes a man desire to do the will of God, and love tells him what that will is.

In writing to correct the error of seeking to attain righteousness by ritual observances, Paul told the Galatians, "For in Christ Jesus neither circumcision nor uncircumcision avails anything, but *faith working through love*" (Galatians 5:6). Actually, we can separate these Christian graces only in thought, for in experience, they blend and interact one with another.

The Roman Catholic idea that "faith is made perfect by love" is actually founded on a mistranslation, for the verb is not in the passive voice, but the middle, as always in the New Testament. Paul is not speaking of faith being perfected; he is declaring that faith is operative: "Faith ... working by love." Faith is an active power. It works. It can function in the supernatural in a most natural fashion. Faith is not merely a passive reliance upon the finished work of Christ or the grace of God, which does everything for us while we luxuriate in inactivity. Faith — active, living faith — goes beyond an intellectual conviction of the truth and begins to operate in its own energy, thereby discovering a field of enterprise in love. Faith shows its energy in love. Even though faith is not the highest of the virtues — love is — still we do not read of love working through faith, but of faith working through love.

As Harold Horton wrote many years ago:

"Faith touches God and brings Him to our aid in every time of need for spirit, soul, or body. Faith invades God's armory for weapons in the fight against sin, storms heaven's strong room for God's promised bestowals. Faith takes God's righteousness for man's sin — and that is salvation. Faith seizes God's fullness for man's emptiness — and that is the baptism in the Holy Spirit. Faith snatches God's health for man's sickness — which is divine healing. Faith grasps God's holiness for man's failure — which is sanctification."

While it is true that faith does grow and finds its perfection in love, it is not the love that produces the faith, but the faith that produces the love. Faith inspires love, as love reciprocally inspires faith. When we believe in and trust the goodness of Christ, we are subsequently moved to love Him.

When David hit his low levels of faith's flow, he turned his attention to loving God, for he had learned that even when he could not trust, he could love. As his love for God began to find expression in praise and song, his faith flow began to spill over the dam and his confidence in God was soon restored.

David activated his faith through obedience

There were times in the life of David when blind obedience released his pent-up faith. With our broader oversight, we understand that the men and women mentioned in the great faith chapter in the Book of Hebrews were all characterized by their implicit obedience to God. A rereading of this eleventh chapter reveals that Abel's sacrifice (Hebrews 11:4) was acceptable to God because he obeyed God in bringing what God had required, while Cain's substitute was totally rejected, and that Noah (Hebrews 11:7) obediently built an ark amidst the mocking of his peers and filled that ark with provisions and animals. He obeyed God in the smallest details even while floating on the flood waters.

David would have known that "by faith Abraham *obeyed* when he was called to go out to the place which he would afterward receive as an inheritance. And he went out, not knowing where he was going" (Hebrews 11:8). Abraham not only went out of Ur in obedience to God's call, he lived a life of obedience with but a few lapses occasioned by his humanity under stress.

The author of the Book of Hebrews merely summarizes the great exploits of faith of these heroes and heroines, but the Old Testament gives us far more details of their activities. The one predominant characteristic found in each of them is *obedience*. They not only believed and trusted in God's word to them; they obeyed it.

The word *obey* is used by the translators of the Old Testament to more fully express the verb *to hear*. It signifies the right response to "the voice" or "the word" of God. "To hear" is to be persuaded, and so to obey. David used this form of speech when speaking of his power as an earthly king: "As soon as they hear of me they obey me; the foreigners submit to me," he wrote (Psalm 18:44). He certainly felt that God deserved the same respect.

To David and the other Old Testament divines, to receive the utterance of God in a noncommittal or merely passive fashion was virtually out of the question. They expected obedience. The only other possibility was active resistance to God's voice, which is called *rebellion* in the Old Testament and *disobedience* in the New Testament.

The patriarchs, prophets and poets of the Old Testament, including David, showed and stated that the proper and fitting response to God's initiative is humble acquiescence that culminates in a combination of active obedience and unconditional trust.

When David's faith hit an all-time low, he stirred it into action by obeying the known will of God. He may not have been hearing a current word from God, which would have given him a fresh flow of faith, but he was capable of continuing to obey the last word he had received. This activated his faith, causing it to break through the rubbish that was holding back the flow of faith.

David activated his faith through action

David knew that faith and obedience could not be separated. As we have already seen, he declared: "I delight to do Your will, O my God, and Your law is within my heart" (Psalm 40:8). David's obedience was not submission to compulsion. He chose to obey with a happy heart.

When my children were at home, it was a satisfying delight for me to have them obey me quickly out of a response of love. "Sure, Daddy, right away," spoken warmly and lovingly, was music equally as beautiful to me as a Brahms' lullaby. When, on the other hand, the response was grudging and obviously said against their will, it was almost as disappointing as disobedience.

If a person finds favor in the tail-wagging, immediate response of the family dog, surely God is satisfied when one of His children reacts to His voice in instant, implicit, inspired obedience. The desire to obey is equal to the deed in the eyes of God, for the set of the soul as it hears God's voice determines the response of the will. The person filled with love for God will be tempered to automatically implement what God has said, while the soul in love with itself will seek to find a way around God's commands. It is nearly the difference between a loving wife responding to her husband's request and a corporate lawyer responding to the most recently passed congressional laws. Some Christians read the Bible in search of those things that would please God, while others study its pages in search of loopholes that could release them from further obligation to obey.

Faith is never inert. Faith is active. The entire faith chapter of Hebrews declares that "by faith" the person did something. Most of the responses were done in obedience to the command of God. The Old Testament repeatedly points out that God does not want mere mechanical or impersonal obedience; God desires obedience from the heart. He yearns for a pattern of response that flows from a fountain of love for God.

David discovered, however, that God speaks not only of health, wealth and happiness, but also of suffering, privation and labor. We cannot pick and choose what we want to obey, for every word of God must be responded to with either a positive or a negative reaction from the hearts of His children. Either we will obey, or we will not. There is no neutral position, nor is there an acceptable substitute for complete obedience. King Saul learned this lesson when he only partially obeyed the Lord and sought to make up for it by offering a massive sacrifice unto God. "Then

Samuel said: 'Has the LORD as great delight in burnt offerings and sacrifices, as in obeying the voice of the LORD? Behold, to obey is better than sacrifice, and to heed than the fat of rams' " (1 Samuel 15:22). Because of this attempt to substitute sacrifice for obedience, God took the kingdom away from Saul and his progeny. Years ago Dr. J.R. Miller said that "it is a great deal easier to do that which God gives us to do, no matter how hard it is, than to face the responsibilities of not doing it." Obedience may be difficult at times, but disobedience is always deadly!

All who have walked with God, or have even seriously read His Word, will agree that not all His commands are pleasant and agreeable. The command for Noah to build an ark carried with it the horrible awareness of the destruction of every living thing that was not in the ark. Abraham must have felt an inner revulsion at God's command to sacrifice Isaac, and Moses had many years of unpleasantness because of God's call to lead the Israelites out of Egypt. But they obeyed anyway, and their obedience activated their faith and became an expression of that faith.

David learned that obedience is a dynamic factor in faith because it activates faith and gives action to an attitude. To declare faith and remain inactive is incongruous. The Christian faith was meant to move us into action. David never viewed his faith as a mental exercise; it was always directions for living. It was his faith that caused him to use his sling against Goliath, for David realized that "faith without works is dead" (James 2:26).

David activated his faith through seeking God

The years of God's provision for David and his 400 men as they lived in the wilderness in caves on the hillsides proved to David that living by faith does not mean doing without, or not doing at all; it means *doing God's will*. Faith is walking with God into new territory as Abraham did. It is obeying God when the request seems incongruous to all known facts, as in Noah's life. It is learning to depend on God rather than developing independence from Him.

Doing God's will and walking with God into new territory requires knowing the will of God. Separated from the priesthood and unable to attend the required feast days, how was David to know God's will for his life?

At least 28 generations after David, Jesus told His disciples, "If anyone wants to do His will, he shall know concerning the doctrine ... " (John 7:17) God accepts the responsibility for making the knowledge of His will available to those who can convince Him that they are prepared to obey it.

In the early days of David's hiding in the cave of Adullam, Abiathar, the sole surviving priest of the massacre at Nob, came to David to tell him that Saul had slain the priests. David urged Abiathar to stay with him as a priest for his men. We read: "Now it happened, when Abiathar the son of Ahimelech fled to David at Keilah, that he went down with an ephod in his hand" (1 Samuel 23:6). In this rescued ephod were the sacred Urim and Thummim by which the priest could inquire of the Lord. The words signify light and perfection, although we are not certain what this refers to.

Many biblical scholars suggest that in the priest's breastplate, or attached to it, were either one or two very beautiful and resplendent diamonds, through which God manifested His will. If the answer to any question reverently put to God by the priest was no, the light in these precious stones dimmed. If the answer was yes, they flashed with splendor.

Whether or not this is the way the Urim and Thummim worked, it must have been a tremendous encouragement to David to have this priceless method of communication between Jehovah and himself. He already had Gad with him as a representative of the prophetic office. Now Abiathar and the ephod brought the priesthood to David. By one or the other of these, David was able to know the will of God at any given moment.

Shortly after Abiathar's arrival, word was brought to David that the Philistines had come to Keilah for plunder. "Therefore David inquired of the LORD, saying, 'Shall I go and attack these Philistines?' And the LORD said to David, 'Go and attack the Philistines, and save Keilah' " (1 Samuel 23:2). When David tried to convince his men to save Keilah, they responded in fear, so David inquired of the Lord a second time. When God again responded positively, the men took courage, overrode their fear with faith and spared the city. Their faith was activated by seeking God's will in the matter.

This was repeated throughout David's life. He would inquire of the Lord before a battle, and even seek God's battleplan. Once David knew the will of God, his faith was on-line and ready for use. Unfortunately for many of us, we do not discipline ourselves to seek the Spirit and the Word (our Urim and Thummim) for guidance when our faith is at its lowest ebb. If we did, it would reactivate our faith. We are ignorant of God's will more often than we rebelliously disobey it. We don't know because we don't ask. David asked, learned and obeyed.

David activated his faith through patience

David not only waited *on* the Lord, he learned to wait *for* Him. He testified: "I waited patiently for the LORD; and He inclined to me, and heard my cry" (Psalm 40:1). David proved that faith is not all action. Sometimes the Lord commands us to "rest in the LORD, and wait patiently for Him; do not fret ..."

(Psalm 37:7) David could not have written this to others if he had not experienced it himself.

Although they often function together, there is a distinct difference between waiting *on* the Lord and waiting *for* Him. We wait on the Lord by prayer, supplication and Bible reading. In so doing, we are looking for the indication of His will. After discovering that will, we must also learn His timing. We wait *for* the Lord by patience and submission; looking for the intervention of His hand in the matter. Faith must have its time of silence, patience and resignation, for true faith is consistently dependent upon God.

In the first eight verses of Psalm 37, his "fret not" psalm, David sandwiches in seven injunctions between two "fret nots," with a third "fret not" added in verse seven. He writes:

Do not fret (verse 1)

(1)   Trust in the Lord, and do good (verse 3)

(2)   Feed on His faithfulness (verse 3)

(3)   Delight yourself also in the Lord (verse 4)

(4)   Commit your way to the Lord (verse 5)

(5)   Rest in the Lord (verse 7)

(6)   Wait patiently for Him (verse 7)

(7)   Cease from anger (verse 8)

Do not fret (verses 7-8)

The long months of waiting took their toll on David's faith, but he had learned to meditate on the Lord — to "feed on His faithfulness" while nothing seemed to be happening. David had a promise and an anointing from God. The throne of Israel was his provisionally, but he waited for it to become his practically.

The time between discovering God's provisional promises and His practical outworking of that promise in our lives can seem interminably long. God has many circumstances to work through to accomplish His purposes. Often He must do a further work in our lives before we are ready to accept the responsibility that goes with those promises. True faith waits for God.

David continued to refuse to lift a finger to secure the kingdom for himself. Jehovah had promised, and David knew that Jehovah would also perform. Divine faith will not allow human intervention into the will of God. God does not tell us to do *for* Him; we are to do *with* Him. This requires the act of waiting patiently until He is ready to function.

David activated his faith through restraint

God's purposes for David required that he be a man of restraint as well as action. "Where the word of a king is, there is power; and who may say to him, 'What are you doing?' " (Ecclesiastes 8:4) Life and death are in the mouth of a king, so there needs to be restraint in his heart. Saul demonstrated how dangerous it is for an unrestrained person to have the power of the kingdom in his hands. God chose to build restraint into David before He gave him the kingdom.

Twice David proved his great self-control when he was given opportunities to kill King Saul. At En Gedi, when Saul and 3,000 men were in hot pursuit of David, this demonized king walked into the very cave in which David and his men were hiding. As Saul stepped out of the blinding glare of the sunshine on the limestone cliffs into the cave, which was as dark as midnight, David and his men, looking toward the mouth of the cave, could see Saul's every action. Saul, however, was unaware of the many eyes staring at him.

When Saul took off his robe and prepared to use the cave for his toilet, David's men whispered, "Seize our opportunity!" It looked like God had given the kingdom to David on his own territory. Somehow

David restrained his men and curbed his own passion that surely burned like fire in every vein in his body. He merely crept close enough to cut off the skirt of the king's robe to prove to him later how completely he had been in David's power.

Much later at Hachilah, David had a second opportunity to slay Saul. Saul was encamped with 3,000 troops. Following the directions of his scouts, David went to inspect this camp from an overhanging cliff. For reasons unknown to us, he proposed to visit the camp and Abishai gladly volunteered to accompany him. God had caused a deep sleep to come upon the camp, so the two men had no difficulty in creeping right to Saul's sleeping form. In hushed whispers, Abishai pled with David, "Let me run him through with his own spear." David refused and instead took the spear and Saul's canteen to a hillside and called for Saul to awaken and send a soldier to retrieve them.

Twice David had Saul in his power, but he restrained himself. He insisted that the death of Saul was in God's hands, not in the hands of David. David would take no advantage of his adversary, neither would he retaliate or avenge his wrong. He refused to believe that opportunity meant permission and license meant liberty. David deliberately chose to wait for the unfolding of the divine purpose, no matter how long it might take.

David's action was courageous. The man who lives in the divine purpose has the secret of unquenchable courage. He relies upon God's promise through the prophet Isaiah:

"No weapon formed against you shall prosper, and every tongue which rises against you in judgment you shall condemn. This is the heritage of the servants of the LORD, and their righteousness is from Me," says the LORD (Isaiah 54:17).

David's faith in God enabled him to fear nothing except doing wrong and grieving Jehovah.

David's great self-restraint and his consistent submission to the will of God inspired his men. Thus, David learned that he won most when he appeared to have yielded most. He gained advantages by refusing to take them wrongfully. He proved that the man who waits for God is a man of power. Others will acknowledge this power and bow beneath his scepter because he waits for God. David learned that submitting to the authority of God's lofty principles brought the benefit of faithful service and implicit obedience from the soldiers who were under him. David's inaction was not a negation of faith. It was a demonstration that great faith inspires others to rise to faith.

Chapter 11

David Inspired Others With His Faith

Faith's Contagion

Ever since it was discovered, the Columbia River has been a source of inspiration to people. It inspired Indians to net and spear the multitudes of salmon that swam up the river to spawn, early settlers to use its waterways for transportation and engineers to capture its force to generate electricity. It has also inspired artists, poets and lovers of all generations. There is something contagious about the silent majesty of the Columbia River.

Similarly, there is something contagious about majestic faith. Just to be around a person with divine faith is an inspiration. It presents itself as a source that will meet our needs. It appears to be a waterway into God's presence. Majestic faith is a source of energy that wants to be harnessed as it moves our souls and brings out the best that is in each of us.

Faith is dangerously infectious. Even an iconoclast doubter isn't safe in the presence of a person of real faith. The officers sent by the chief priests and Pharisees to arrest Jesus returned empty handed with the report, " 'No man ever spoke like this Man!' Then the Pharisees answered them, 'Are you also deceived?' " (John 7:46-47) These doubters began to doubt their doubts when they encountered divine faith. It still happens. Faith continues to be contagious and inspiring. Faith dares to believe beyond present circumstances, and in doing so, entices others to also reach beyond the seen into the unseen.

Faith's inspiration of displaying

Few persons ever come into a new position or experience with God without first seeing it in the life of another. For every person that God can move into a fresh walk of faith, there are a thousand who cannot see beyond their present experiences. For sheep are near-sighted, and the Bible likens believers to sheep. God needs a few people who can see beyond their peers and move into greater realms of God's grace, for He knows that near-sighted sheep tend to follow anything that moves.

In the New Testament, faith is listed as a fruit of the Holy Spirit (see Galatians 5:22,23). The faith spoken of here is not regarded as the means of salvation or as the instrument of our justification, but as the principle of Christian life that controls and guides it. Some translators have substituted the word *faithful* for *faith* in the list of the gifts, but this is not consistent with the Greek text. Besides, *being faithful* is not synonymous with *having faith*, for faith is a divine energy, while faithfulness and fidelity are actions or responses.

Furthermore, we can develop or produce *faithfulness* through discipline and self-control, but no person can produce *faith*. We can but bear it. Faith is a force; faithfulness is the flow. Faith is the action, while faithfulness is the reaction. We need to be on guard lest we seek to produce the cause instead of the effect, for faith is the cause and our faithfulness, fidelity or trustfulness is but an effect of that faith. Whenever we try to produce what only God can produce, we meet with frustration and failure.

By placing faith on the list of the fruits of the Spirit, the Holy Spirit reveals to us that there is an inner working, a progressive dealing of Himself within our lives, that contributes to the operation of divine faith. Faith is not only a force without us; it is a force within us. It is both obtainable by the Christian and observable by his or her friends. Faith is, indeed, an acquired grace, but it becomes an adorning grace as well. While it is a strength to the possessor, it is a stimulant to the observer that will often create an appetite for that fruit.

The Holy Spirit causes us to become fruitful in our relationships with God, others and ourselves. He makes us to be a fragrant aroma, a stimulating sight and a satisfying flavor to Him who is above us, those who are around us, and the one who is with us. The fruit of the Spirit in our lives effect blessings to God, beneficence to our fellow creatures, and benefits to ourselves.

Obviously, the Christian does not produce this fruit; he bears it. It is not a human endeavor aided by the Spirit, but a divine enablement submitted to by Christian believers. Each may bear the fruit, but none can produce it.

In speaking of faith as a fruit of the Spirit, Paul not only makes it obvious that only Christians bear this fruit, though they do not produce it, but he also shows that faith is not solely for the person who possesses it. No tree eats its own fruit. The vine bears grapes for persons to eat. Similarly, Christians bear fruit for others to "taste and see that the LORD is good" (Psalm 34:8).

Marketing experts discovered long ago that one taste is worth pages of pictures and descriptions. Therefore, they began to send smiling women into the marketplace with free samples of their new foods to demonstrate the new product. One taste of a portion stuck on the end of a toothpick usually was sufficient to create an appetite and a desire for the product. Similarly, God delights to put the fruit of faith into the lives of believers and send them into the marketplace as free samples of the goodness of God.

Fresh, ripe, aromatic fruit has a way of stirring the gastric juices in the stomach and creating an appetite. Furthermore, since fruit is not ingested by the plant, but is grown for consumption by those who cannot produce fruit, others get their first taste of the divine realm from association with fruit-bearing Christians. Our freshly ripened faith creates a hunger, and fortunately, the same fruit that creates hunger is satisfied by faith.

David was one such demonstrator. He so displayed the fruit of faith during the fearful times in his life that those who lived with him could smell it and taste it. Inspired by their leader, David's men also desired divine faith. Because they had seen it at work in David, they were inspired to reach Godward for their own faith.

Faith's inspiration of daring

What unlocks faith in one person may not touch a second individual. A few years ago, in a vision, a pastor petitioned the Lord to specially bless three of the outstanding saints in his congregation. Jesus agreed to do so. As the three stood by the altar at the front of the church, Jesus walked by the first saint, stood near the second, and reached out to touch the third.

"This third Christian must have great faith," the pastor said.

"No," Jesus answered. "The first person sensed My presence the moment I walked into the room. The second needed the nearness of My presence, but this third person had to be touched by Me to unlock faith in My presence." Jesus gave the measure of faith that was commensurate with the need.

David discovered that it is not always the attitude of faith that inspires others. Many need to see that faith in action before they are stirred to function in God's faith. For them, words are less effective than deeds.

When young David dared to accept the challenge of Goliath, his faith in action inspired King Saul. Because he had been successful over a bear and a lion in the name of the Lord, David was confident that he would be successful over this Philistine challenger. The logic of this allusion isn't too sound, for Goliath was a far greater threat than any predator animal David had faced as a shepherd boy. But David's faith so inspired Saul that he risked his kingdom to let David fight Goliath. Israel needed someone with a daring courage. David was the only person around who possessed it.

Similarly, David's perilous venture into Saul's camp to capture the king's spear and canteen was a bold act that inspired his men and caused the camp of Israel to fear. David later learned that this one act of courage had both inspired his followers and terrorized the enemy. So it is with Christians. Nothing disturbs our spiritual enemy more than to see us step out in daring faith, for it is positive proof that we possess more than a mental concept of faith. We have a divine energy flowing in our spirits.

It is easy to back away saying, "I'm just not naturally a courageous person," but the fruit of the Spirit (which includes divine faith) do not spring from anything inherent within us. They are the result of the new life flowing through us from the Holy Spirit. Courageous faith is not a product of our minds or our emotions; it is a result of the presence of the Third Person of the Trinity within our lives. We only need to remain in an intimate, abiding connection with Christ

Jesus, who is the vine, to enjoy a production of the fruit of faith. This faith in us will induce a challenge that entices others to join us in our faith.

When we were children, it was common for us to dare one of the group to do something that was either dangerous or prohibited. If the dare was accepted, the rest of us were awestruck. After the fact, however, we often joined in and participated in the "success" of the dare. David seemed to inspire others to develop a daring attitude.

David knew that the source of his courageous faith was not inherent, for twice he cried: "Be of good courage, and He shall strengthen your heart" (Psalms 27:14 and 31:24). Jehovah was the source of his courage. God's divine faith flowed in David's inner being. David's psalms reveal his knowledge that the gift of faith may take the form of an inner illumination, an active assurance, a continuing calmness or a pulsating power. In some manner it gives the participant a physical or emotional evidence of its presence.

This divine faith that made David so daring is generally accompanied by inner peace, calmness and tranquility. It is very much like the eye of the hurricane, where there is calm in the midst of a devastating storm. When the gift of faith is functioning, the believer is as assured of a change in the situation as though it had already transpired, although there may be a lengthy time delay between the operation of the gift and the actualization of that gift. This level of faith knows that it knows and what it knows, although it is often hard pressed to explain why it knows. David's faith was a gift from God. It was not a leap in the dark or a crawling out on a limb. It was a moving into perfect harmony with the will of God, even though that will was still an unexplained factor. While David did not know all the facts, he knew Jehovah and he had an inner assurance from Him that everything was under divine control. This made it easy for David to function in a daring manner that, in turn, became an amazing inspiration for others to join him.

Faith's inspiration of desiring

Recognizing the inspiration of daring to accomplish some goal is easier than appreciating the incentive of desire, but this strong, inner motivation that creates dreams is essential to leadership. Faith becomes eyes to the soul that enable a person to see beyond the present into the distant future. David had such eyes. He was a dreamer, but his dreams were not fantasies. They became driving desires that motivated his life. After he had invested years as king over all Israel, David, speaking of himself in the third person, told God: "You have given him his heart's desire, and have not withheld the request of his lips. Selah" (Psalm 21:2). Placid acceptance of the status quo is not the way faith operates. David learned that divine faith creates inner cravings that are far higher than present circumstances. He was familiar with Joseph's dreams that became a pulsating passion in his life. Those dreams were followed by a pit, Potiphar's house, an Egyptian prison and finally Pharaoh's throne. David remembered that Joseph's faith had started with a dream. In like manner, David dreamed with great desire.

This king's desires did not come from a lust for power or a need for greatness. His dreams were inspired by God's anointing. Long before Paul wrote it, David experienced that "... it is God who works in you both to will and to do for His good pleasure" (Philippians 2:13). The desires in David's life were divinely inspired. They were the inner workings of faith, for God had caused David to desire to do what He wanted.

These burning aspirations in David became an inspiration for those around him. They saw that he desired, he set out to accomplish and he succeeded. David and those who gathered around him were completely successful in hiding from King Saul. Although he had his heart set upon the throne and he had been crowned king over Judah, David did not rest contentedly until he was crowned king over all Israel. This was the anointed dream that God had placed in his life. He never lost that vision.

There must have been times when David's mighty men talked of going back to their homes, but David's dream continued to inspire their hearts for a kingdom of righteous government. For David there could be no turning back. He had but one gear in his life, and that was full speed forward! His momentum carried others along with him.

Perhaps the most notable incident that shows how infectious David's desires became to those who were close to him was his desire for a drink from the well at Bethlehem. Shortly after he had been crowned king over all Judah, the Philistines challenged him with a full-scale attack. Indeed, they attacked in such vast numbers that they cut off David's connection with the northern tribes and forced him to retreat from Hebron, where he had been reigning as king in comparative peace and security.

David fled to the fortress cave of Adullam, where he had so successfully hidden from King Saul. Many years had passed since he had used the cave as his headquarters. Being here again must have invoked many memories. Although his flight to the cave was a tremendous set-back for David — a complete reversal of fortune — David did not lose his desire. Once again, he cast himself upon Jehovah. He was confident that the God who had set him on the throne could keep him on the throne, Philistines or no Philistines.

While David ordered his forces from his cave headquarters, many of his men distinguished themselves in the battle. Abishai, the son of Zeruiah, smote the giant who, with his new sword, almost slew David. Elhanan slew the brother of Goliath of Gath, and Jonathan, David's nephew, slew a huge monstrosity who had defied Israel. These feats of valor were inspired by the faith of David. It is amazing what can be done by the inspiration of a single life! Fifteen or so years earlier, David had challenged and defeated Goliath in this same territory. Now men gathered around him and, inspired by his faith, encouraged him to stay in the cave and leave the fighting to them.

Adullam is not far from Bethlehem where David had led his father's flocks to pasture in the valleys where he was not fighting. Memories came swooping back from the past. One sultry afternoon when he was a semi-prisoner in the cave, there came an irresistible longing to taste the water of the well of Bethlehem. Almost involuntarily "... David said with longing, 'Oh, that someone would give me a drink of the water from the well of Bethlehem, which is by the gate!' " (2 Samuel 23:15) He was unaware that his men had over heard him, nor did he suspect that his men would be foolhardy enough to risk their lives just to get him a drink. But "... three mighty men broke through the camp of the Philistines, drew water from the well of Bethlehem that was by the gate, and took it and brought it to David. Nevertheless he would not drink it, but poured it out to the LORD" (2 Samuel 23:16).

That water was a priceless expression of a love that was stronger than death. David could not drink it. He poured it out as a libation offering to God saying, "Far be it from me, O LORD, that I should do this! Is this not the blood of the men who went in jeopardy of their lives?" (2 Samuel 23:17)

Where did such courage come from? It was inspired by David's faith. These men had so come to trust the deep longings in David's heart that they responded in faith to this simple request, believing that if David desired it, God must have ordained it, and thus He would enable them to perform it. Was this desire inspired of God? We'll never know. What we do know is that this expressed longing stirred faith in these warriors. Deep yearnings are often the tool God uses to inspire faith in others.

Faith's inspiration of worshiping

The ultimate desire of David's heart was to worship Jehovah. He cried: "One thing I have desired of the LORD, that will I seek: that I may dwell in the house of the LORD all the days of my life, to behold the beauty of the LORD, and to inquire in His temple" (Psalm 27:4). David was a worshiper long before God inspired his dreams of becoming a king. To his credit, he never allowed this dream to turn him away from his earlier desires. The conscious presence of Jehovah meant more to David than dominion, authority and power.

On the very eve of his ascension to the throne, David almost lost it all. After sneaking into Saul's camp to take his spear and canteen, David got tired of hiding. He again approached the king of Gath and requested asylum. King Achish granted his request and gave David and his company the city of Ziklag for their headquarters (1 Samuel 27:6). David lived here for 16 months while raiding the Geshurites, the Gizrites and the Amalekites. When Saul heard that David was living in Gath, he raised an army to attack the Philistines. David and his men were summoned by King Achish to serve as his personal bodyguards. This did not meet with the approval of the other lords of the Philistines, and David and his men were dismissed and told to return home.

Pretending to be incensed at this insult, David and his men marched three days to Ziklag, only to find that the Amalekites had captured the city, sacked it and burned it to the ground (1 Samuel 30:1). Although this is what David and his men had been doing to the Amalekites, it was their first experience of having it done to them. "Then David and the people who were with him lifted up their voices and wept, until they had no more power to weep" (1 Samuel 30:4). Their wives and children had been taken captive, and their homes and possessions had been destroyed. The grief proved to be overwhelming to these men who had undergone such hardships for many years.

> *Then David was greatly distressed, for the people spoke of stoning him, because the soul of all the people was grieved, every man for his sons and his daughters. But David strengthened himself in the LORD his God* (1 Samuel 30:6).

It is painful to have people turn against your leadership, but the pain is overwhelming when it is the very people in whom you have invested years of your life.

The pain and grief in his men cost David his leadership, and almost cost him his life. A vote was taken to decide whether or not to stone David. While the men could think only of projecting blame and seeking vengeance, David turned his thoughts to the Lord. Surely God's promises could not be thwarted now. He had come too far for defeat. "David strengthened himself in the Lord his God." What a demonstration of faith in the midst of trouble.

Worship is never based on circumstances. It is always a response to an unchanging God. David recognized that God's nature and His goodness were unaltered by this attack. It was only David's situation that had changed. David reasoned that if the men did, indeed, decide to stone him, he could not successfully defend himself. If he was to die, he wanted to die worshiping Jehovah.

This expression of faith stopped the men in their tracks. Once again there was a contagion of faith. David called for Abiathar the priest to bring the ephod and to inquire of the Lord as to whether or not they should pursue the Amalekites. The Lord told them to pursue, and He promised them complete victory. They pursued and recovered everything they had lost, plus the spoil these Amalekites had taken from other raids.

While this was going on, the war against Israel was in full swing. King Saul had sought out the witch at En Dor, asked her to bring up Samuel and inquired of Samuel whether he would be victorious. He was told that he had but one day to live, and it proved to be true. A chance arrow in the battle found its mark, hitting Saul, who then fell on his own sword and died. Within days, David was crowned king in Hebron.

Once again David proved that worship is where the kingdom of God starts, before it flows out into transformed families, businesses and societies. It was this act of worshiping in the face of complete defeat that inspired his men to go once more into battle, the final battle before David's kingship.

If David had not been a worshiper, he might have perished on the eve of his coronation. Because he worshiped, he inspired his men to join him in renewed faith in Jehovah. With their attention drawn from their negative circumstances to God's positive presence, their courage returned and God restored to them everything they had lost and more.

Only a worshiper can lead others into worship, for it is not the action of worship, but the flow of faith in worship, that reaches the hearts of nonworshipers and challenges them to submit themselves to Almighty God. What a privilege it is not only to possess divine faith but to display it in such a way as to inspire others into the flow of that faith.

Chapter 12

David Maintained His Faith

Faith's Permanence

Unlike the Salt River in Arizona that flows only after a heavy rain, the Columbia River has maintained its flow through centuries. Its source, Lake Columbia, feeds a consistent volume of water regardless of the weather, and the seven major rivers that flow into the Columbia drain over 85 percent of the northwestern United States. Drought in one area is generally offset by rain in another. Although there is a seasonal fluctuation in the water level, the river flows on through the four seasons of the year.

In contrast to the Columbia, many of God's children flow their faith only in the season of God's rain. When revival is in the land, they flow like the Salt River. They even break over their banks and flood others around them. They are a source of blessing to everyone around them and it appears that they have come into a great ministry. But since they have only the rains for their source, they quickly degenerate into a dry riverbed when the season of revival ends. They have never tapped into God on a personal level, nor have they learned how to maintain their faith.

David was more like the Columbia River than the Salt River. He found a renewable source of faith. He maintained his access to the faith of God that enabled him to flow both in the times of spiritual rain and in dry times of apostasy.

David *bought* his faith

The contrast between King Saul and King David is broad and varied. There is enough dissimilarity to fill a book. This distinction is especially obvious in the way each handled the faith that God imparted to them. Saul needed the special intervention of Samuel to explain God's plan for his life. He had such difficulty accepting this that God gave him special signs to confirm it. In considerable detail, God spoke through Samuel to tell Saul he would meet two men by Rachel's tomb who would tell him that his father's donkeys had been found and his father was worried about him. Next he was told:

> *Then you shall go on forward from there and come to the terebinth tree of Tabor. There three men going up to God at Bethel will meet you, one carrying three young goats, another carrying three loaves of bread, and another carrying a skin of wine* (1 Samuel 10:3).

This was certainly specific, but there was more.

> *After that you shall come to the hill of God where the Philistine garrison is. And it will happen, when you have come there to the city, that you will meet a group of prophets coming down from the high place with a stringed instrument, a tambourine, a flute, and a harp before them; and they will be prophesying. Then the Spirit of the LORD will come upon you, and you will prophesy with them and be turned into another man. And let it be, when these signs come to you, that you*

do as the occasion demands; for God is with you
(1 Samuel 10:5-7).

This came to pass exactly as Samuel declared it would (see 1 Samuel 10:9). God was raining faith into Saul's heart.

In contrast to this, David paid a price for his faith. He contacted God while tending sheep on the hillsides of Bethlehem. His faith in God was tested repeatedly. First, in the matter of the lion and the bear, then in meeting the challenge of Goliath. When he was anointed by Samuel to become king over Israel, no one gathered around him. No signs and wonders accompanied or immediately followed the anointing as had happened to Saul. Instead of being acknowledged as king, he was selected to be the court musician. When it looked like things were moving toward his leadership, David was driven from the palace to the wilderness by Saul's anger. There David's faith was tested.

While David was developing and enlarging his faith through constant trials, King Saul was drying up like Arizona's Salt River. David was learning to live by faith, while Saul was learning to live without faith. Each received the same calling and anointing; each was endowed by God with a living faith. But Saul never learned to maintain that faith. He compromised in his obedience, he lied to God's prophet, and he became greedy and overbearing in his leadership. Instead of remaining the channel of anointed leadership that God had intended, he became a selfish self-centered despot who denied God's faith so completely that when he needed supernatural guidance, he sought out a witch to contact demon spirits on his behalf.

David not only maintained his contact with the source of his faith — Jehovah — he allowed that faith to be increased by the additional flow of lesser streams that came into his life. He found strength in the 400 men who came to him. He kept a prophet and a priest with him all the days of his wanderings, and he inquired of God through them regularly. When he was quickly entreated by Abigail, the wife of Nabal (see 1 Samuel 25), David responded to her plea with the words: "... Blessed be the LORD God of Israel, who sent you this day to meet me!" (1 Samuel 25:32)

Since David bought his faith through adversity and personal involvement, he chose to maintain it. Life consistently reveals that what is received without cost is treated lightly. How often a large inheritance has destroyed a young person. "Easy come; easy go" is applicable in both the natural and the spiritual. Saul received his faith as a gift from God, but he didn't find it valuable enough to maintain it. David felt very differently about his faith. It came the hard way, and he held onto it until he died.

This same contrast can be seen in the Church today. Those who receive faith, ministries and special gifts without much personal involvement — by the laying on of hands, for instance — often don't care enough about these blessings to maintain them. Or they have no idea how to maintain them, so it's "easy come; easy go."

David never *departed from* the faith

Those who search for apparent contradictions in the Bible enjoy pointing out two conflicting verses in the writings of Paul. Paul declared to the church at Rome: "... God has dealt to each one a measure of faith" (Romans 12:3), but Paul said to the church in Thessalonica: "... for not all have faith" (2 Thessalonians 3:2). Actually, this is not a contradiction, but a comparison. While it is true that God, in His mercy, gives all persons a measure of faith, it is equally true that many of them, like King Saul before them, do not nurture and maintain this faith. The world has always had an abundance of Hymenaeuses and

Alexanders who "... concerning the faith have suffered shipwreck" (1 Timothy 1:19).

No person has ever been destroyed by God's faith, for divine faith brings life, not death. But many who began in faith, ended in apostasy, a word that means "renunciation of a religious faith" or "defection." What they once revered, they renounced. They defected from that in which they had once delighted. Faith became a fallacy for them. Although they once relied on it, now they rebel at it. They have become apostate to the faith.

Some have abandoned the very truth in which they abode because they never found true, divine faith. They embraced a pseudo faith — a doctrinal concept — without a divine commitment. Thus, when they could not make it work for them, they deserted it. Theirs was a conscious, deliberate forsaking of something that proved to be false.

A great number of people get involved in apostasy even after they have been partakers of and participants in God's true divine faith. Usually, like King Saul, their recantation is subtle. It is more a work of their subconscious than conscious minds. This apostasy is seldom a deliberate renunciation of faith, but more likely is an insidious replacement of that faith.

In Paul's first letter to Timothy, he lists five ways people who once walked in faith end up bankrupt of faith. He declares, first, that some *depart* from the faith: "Now the Spirit expressly says that in latter times some will depart from the faith ... " (1 Timothy 4:1) In the first three verses of First Timothy, chapter four, Paul lists five reasons for this departure from faith:

(1)   Heeding seducing spirits

(2)   Observing doctrines of devils

(3)   Deceitful hypocrisy

(4)   Prohibiting marriage

(5)   Banning the eating of certain foods

The generation of Christians to whom Paul presented the message of the gospel was very new, and they lacked the New Testament to guide them. Nevertheless, their departure from the faith has not been unique. Today's generation of Christians has all the advantages of Bibles, churches, Christian radio and television, religious books and a seemingly endless supply of pastors, yet they still suffer from this same malady. Extreme concern with the demonic has caused many to depart from the faith, as has unreasonable asceticism in the matters of marriage and permissible foods. Such individuals allow themselves to get caught up in rules and trivialities until something short of God, who alone is "the author and finisher of our faith" (Hebrews 12:2), becomes the center of their lives.

Saul's involvement with the demonic was the reason God slayed him. David, on the other hand, never showed an interest in the doctrines of devils. He was so comfortable with his relationship with God that he just ignored the devil. As a result, he never departed from the faith.

David never *denied* his faith

The second way apostasy grips the hearts of individuals is through their failure or refusal to meet their family responsibilities. Paul told Timothy: "But if anyone does not provide for his own, and especially for those of his household, he has *denied* the faith and is worse than an unbeliever" (1 Timothy 5:8). Denial of the faith, as Paul sees it, is not only a negative confession but an unwillingness to provide support for the family.

During the gracious flow of life known as the Charismatic renewal, there was a surprisingly high incidence of individuals who wanted to "live by faith," which often turned out to be little more than bumming a living off the church. Refusing to work so one can have more time for Bible reading and prayer is not living by faith; it is *denial* of faith. In my book *Let Us Abide*, I wrote:

"When Paul wrote his epistle to the church at Thessalonica, he found it necessary to say: 'But we beseech you, brethren ... that you study (Greek, "be ambitious") to be quiet, and to *do your own business*, and to *work with your own hands*, as we have commanded you; that ye may walk honestly toward them that are without, and *that ye have lack of nothing*' (1 Thessalonians 4:10-12). It would seem that even in his day, there were some who had to be admonished to go to work. I guess the concept that the world owes us a living isn't so new after all. Laziness is inherent in most of our natures, and unless we conquer it, it will control us. In a day when welfare, unemployment payments, disability insurance, and guaranteed income are so available, the lazy man can make a career of doing nothing and depending upon society to provide for him ... But the Bible does not make society responsible for the lazy and indigent. It merely offers work for the able and aid for the poor."

When Saul became king, he sat back expecting the people over whom he reigned to provide for his needs. He lived sumptuously even though the taxation was ruining many of the people of the land. Most of the 400 men who quickly joined David at the Adullam cave were seriously in debt to Saul because of their inability to pay these taxes. Their property had already been confiscated, and they were in danger of imprisonment or death.

In contrast, David not only supplied his own needs during this same period of time, he accepted responsibility for his parents, the priest and the prophet who ministered unto him, and these 400 men who had come to him. He extended his faith to cover everyone who shared in his "family." He never denied his faith. He used it to bless others.

We often ignore the principle that God gives to us so we are able to give to others. Whenever we try to contain all that God gives, the flow stops. We are never to become repositories for God's faith. He has chosen us to be channels through which that faith can flow. We are rivers, not lakes. David consistently flowed his faith to others — not only in material blessings but in song, psalms and exhortation.

David never *cast off* his faith

Paul taught that a third way people lose their God-given faith is to "... *cast off* their first faith" (1 Timothy 5:12). He relates this to younger widows who "grow wanton against Christ" (1 Timothy 5:11). The expression, *grow wanton*, refers to passion or sensual desires. Satan likes to stir inordinate sexual desire in faithful believers, for he knows the power this drive exerts on the human nature.

The first group Paul spoke of *departed* from the faith by forbidding marriage; this group *cast off* their faith to embrace sensual pleasure. Any time sensual desire is given expression outside the channels of marriage, it becomes such an enemy to our faith that we will cast off either our immorality or our faith.

David learned this the hard way. When his lust for Bathsheba caused him to commit adultery, he lost the abiding presence of Jehovah that had been his experience from youth. When he finally got around to repenting for this sin, he cried: "Create in me a clean heart, O God, and renew a steadfast spirit within me.

Do not cast me away from Your presence, and do not take Your Holy Spirit from me" (Psalm 51:10-11). David quickly learned that the temporary sensual pleasure he had derived by having another man's wife as a sex partner could not be compared to the cost of losing God's presence. His faith was more valuable to him than sexual satisfaction.

The amoral attitude America has taken toward sex is already causing many people to *cast off* their faith. Look at the list of fallen preachers, divorced elders and deacons, and joyless people in the pews of our churches. Oh, they may not cease to attend church. To the contrary, we now have special churches for those living in open immorality. Fornicators, adulterers, homosexuals and lesbians are now being ordained to the ministry by some religious groups. They deny the Bible's standard of sexual behavior and refer to their lifestyle as "alternate." God refers to it as an *abomination.*

They may assemble and participate in religious activities, but there is no divine faith among them. The power of God is not present to transform lives. They display no evangelistic power. The gospel they proclaim is a false gospel, and they worship "another Jesus" (2 Corinthians 11:4). The sick do not get healed, and if a dead person were restored to life, it would seriously scare them. Paul defines them as a people "... having a form of godliness but denying its power. And from such people turn away!" (2 Timothy 3:5)

These sexually promiscuous persons who seek the cover of religion for their activities have *cast off* their first faith. In order to embrace an unscriptural sex life, they released their faith in the inspired Word of God and in the claims of the God of that inspiration. It is a flinging to the winds of faith in order to have a fling in sensuality. What a price to pay for temporary pleasure!

Some have even dared point to David as an excuse for their immoral behavior, but they are unfairly ignoring David's confession, repentance and turning from immorality. The Bible speaks of only one incidence of adultery in David's life. He walked in the faith he had received from God and lived a pure life by the standards of God's revelation to that generation. In doing so, he did not *cast off* his faith.

David never *turned aside* from his faith

The fourth way people lose their faith, according to the apostle Paul, is to "*turn aside* after satan" (1 Timothy 5:15). Our first thoughts probably go back to Saul who turned to witchcraft when Samuel was gone and the priesthood could not (or would not, because of the slaughter at the priestly city of Nob) contact God for him. This was an overt *turning aside* from his faith.

The context of Paul's letter, however, does not speak of witchcraft or satanic worship. It speaks about idleness, gossiping, talebearing and busybody activities. This, the Spirit says, is demonic activity. Paul's answer to this was to urge marriage, the bearing of children, and the proper care of the house. Idleness becomes the spawning ground for much mischief. While our society is clamoring for more and more free time, it is also *turning aside* from faith. In many recreational areas, pastors secretly rejoice at inclement weather on Sunday, for it usually means a larger attendance at the Sunday services, inasmuch as there is nowhere else to go in a rainstorm.

Many Christians who embraced faith in poverty, turn aside from it in times of plenty! Any pastor could give you the names of people who have turned to God's divine faith in a time of desperate need, but who turned aside from it when their problems were relieved. It is not so much that God is undesirable. It is that other things become even more desirable.

When it is a choice between God's faith and man's fun, faith generally gets *turned aside*.

During the years of his hiding and running from Saul, David kept himself busily engaged. He survived because he maintained his faith. When Israel crowned him king over all twelve tribes, David did not sit back and take it easy. He led Israel's army in battle after battle as he enlarged her borders and secured her peace. He rebuilt the worship structure of the nation. He wrote psalms and revitalized and realigned the priesthood. He invented new musical instruments, organized choirs, established an orchestra to play before Jehovah and returned the Ark to Jerusalem. David never rested in his laurels. After successfully accomplishing one task, he set his heart to another. He seemed to realize that an idle mind is the devil's workshop. He became a highly respected statesman, as well as a cunning warrior. He was an honest judge and a faithful king. He learned to channel the faith he gained in adversity to quality living in prosperity.

Perhaps if more of us could learn this lesson, fewer of us would continue to live in hostile circumstances. When God sees that our faith remains consistent only under pressure, He is most capable of maintaining a high level of pressure to keep us in faith. When we mature sufficiently to maintain high faith levels in times of rest, security and sufficiency, God may remove some of the pressure from our lives.

God wants retired people to live in the same vibrant faith they had when they were part of the working force. He never wants His children to trust in riches, retirement programs or Social Security. He is always the source of supply for our lives, whether it is during our childbearing years or our final years of relaxation. David kept the faith for his entire life.

David never *strayed* from the faith

Paul wrote of two groups who *erred from the faith*. The first group erred from the faith in covetousness over money. He wrote: "For the love of money is a root of all kinds of evil, for which some have *strayed from the faith* in their greediness, and pierced themselves through with many sorrows" (1 Timothy 6:10).

The love of money and materialism have caused many to err from the faith. In so doing they have "pierced themselves through with many sorrows." If a love for things is the breeding ground for many sorrows and an occasion to err or stray from the faith, what a shame that the attainment of wealth is set forth as a motivating force to get people interested in faith in the first place. They are promised whatever they can believe for, but when their lust levels rise, they find that they have "wandered away from the faith," as many modern translations put it. Then all they retain is the love of money and hearts broken from many sorrows.

The second group wandered from the faith through intellectualism. Paul's warning is as follows:

> *O Timothy! Guard what was committed to your trust, avoiding the profane and vain babblings and contradictions of what is falsely called knowledge — by professing it, some have strayed concerning the faith. Grace be with you. Amen* (1 Timothy 6:20-21).

Godless talk and foolish arguments with those who boast of their knowledge can sidetrack us from really knowing God, which is the ultimate purpose of faith.

That David was the most brilliant man of his generation is beyond question. His psalms reveal this. This never turned him from his faith in God, for he saw God as the source of his knowledge. Everything he knew and learned turned him back to God, not away from Him. He, unlike our generation, did not place science as a substitute for God. He felt that everything he discovered about life and nature helped him to better understand the Creator.

There is no question that "... God has dealt to each one a measure of faith" (Romans 12:3), for natural life is seriously impaired without it, and salvation is impossible when it is not present. But not all men have faith. Some have *departed* from faith; others have *denied* the faith; still others have *cast off*, *turned aside*, and *wandered from* the faith that was given to them. In every instance, their loss of faith was the result of a positive action or attitude: refusal to work, lust, idleness, materialism or intellectualism. It was never a direct refutation of that faith, but a replacement of their faith with something else. Maintaining faith requires maturing in our relationship with God. Anything that replaces that relationship also replaces our faith.

Can anyone live in a decadent society such as ours and maintain the level of faith that God committed to him? Noah did, Abraham did, Moses did, and, very obviously, David did. They lived in evil times with far less light than we possess. Yet the eleventh chapter of Hebrews shows them, and many others, maintaining their faith in God and His promises in the midst of circumstances worse than we face. The secret seems to be their intimate relationship with God. They did not increase their faith by planting it like a seed, but by faithfully praying to God. They did not maintain their faith through works, but through worship. They didn't spend their days claiming the promise, but in celebrating the One who did the promising.

It is likely that unless we return to their values and emulate their actions, we may end up in unmitigated apostasy rather than unfeigned faith. Peter declared that we "... have obtained like precious faith ... by the righteousness of our God and Savior Jesus Christ" (2 Peter 1:1). God grant us such a warm relationship with Him that we will never obscure this precious faith we have obtained from Him. It is in our power to be apostolic in our faith or apostate to that faith.

Chapter 13

David Lived in His Faith

Faith's Continuity

When it is time for the salmon to spawn, the Columbia River seems alive with fish fighting their way upstream to the place where, several years before, they had hatched. The fish ladders that bypass the dams often overwhelm the salmon fighting to rise above this man-made obstacle. As they leap from one level to another, some make it the first time. Many fall back and have to reposition themselves for another try. It is exhausting work, and many salmon never make it to the top of the ladder.

During the years that I lived along the Columbia River, I greatly enjoyed watching the Indians netting and spearing salmon during this season of the year. They positioned themselves on rocks in the rapids or on makeshift platforms that they had constructed at the base of the fish ladders. During this short spawning season, they took thousands of pounds of fish out of the river. They sold some to tourists, but most of their catch was dried or smoked, and saved for their winter food supply.

Only the Indians are allowed to fish this way. It is part of their treaty with the United States. The rest of us have to use a rod and a reel. The Columbia River can yield an annual supply of 4,500,000 pounds of salmon. That is a lot of fish for one river, but the Columbia is their natural habitat and home.

David lived in his faith

While in one sense we think of faith as a river that flows through the life of an individual, in another sense we see that a person can actually live in that river of faith. David was such a person. Far more than possessing faith, he inhabited it. He lived in it and breathed it. Faith was the source of life for him. He could go upstream in his faith and find God, or he could go downstream and find an abundant life.

Many years after David died, a prophet named Habakkuk came on the scene of Israel's history. He was familiar with David's life. This minor prophet may have picked his ideas of faith from the great psalmist of Israel. While standing in his watchtower and seeking Jehovah during an invasion of Israel by the Chaldeans, Habakkuk received a vision involving the end times. God told him in this divine visitation that "... the just shall live by his faith" (Habakkuk 2:4). Before receiving this revelation, Habakkuk was depressed and very accusative of God for allowing this invasion. After God imparted this truth into his heart, his attitude changed and he offered a prayer that was to be sung with a double harp, so great was the excitement this insight produced in him.

Many generations later, God quickened this truth to the heart of a Roman Catholic priest named Martin Luther. It became the touchstone of the Reformation: *The just shall live by faith.* It is not merely that those whom Christ has justified will be possessors of faith, but that they will productively live in their faith.

Faith, therefore, becomes more than a force; it is a focus. Likewise, faith is far more than a channel through which we receive gifts. It is a calling in which we respond to God. We live, not lust, by faith. Faith is more a walk than a work. It is a way of living that is assured in the Old Testament and reassured three times in the New Testament.

"For in it the righteousness of God is revealed from faith to faith; as it is written, 'The just shall live by faith,' " Paul wrote (Romans 1:17). The emphasis in this context is on *the just*. Not all shall live by faith, but "the just" — those who have accepted the finished work of Christ Jesus as redemption for their sins — shall "live by faith." What began as a work of faith will be lived out as a walk of faith. The process is *from* faith *to* faith. This walk of faith is progressive and continuous, past and contemporary. He who declared us *just* has decreed a life of faith. They go together like fish and water.

Paul wrote to the church in Galatia that was striving with legalism and works: "But that no one is justified by the law in the sight of God is evident, for *'The just shall live by faith'* " (Galatians 3:11). By quoting Habakkuk in his letter to the Galatians, Paul seems to emphasize the words *shall live*. Paul had told them earlier, "... I live by faith in the Son of God, who loved me and gave Himself for me" (Galatians 2:20). Now Paul is directing them to stop trying to live by the law and to learn to live by God's faith.

In *Let Us Abide*, I wrote:

"The life of faith is not optional; it is obligatory. God has never offered it as an elective for the super saints. It is not a matter of preference; it is a prerequisite to divine life. Therefore, great portions of the Old Testament reveal, often in painstaking detail, the steps God used to develop a life and the walk of faith in His men."

This is why so many chapters of the Old Testament chronicle the life of David. He was a man who first developed a life of faith, then lived his life in that faith.

He came to know his God, and he learned to live in an extremely close relationship with Him.

It is God's will that we "*live* by faith," not merely subsist by faith. Since Jesus declared, "I have come that they may have life, and that they may have it more abundantly" (John 10:10), we gather that to *live by* faith is to live abundantly, with nothing lacking. While living by faith may include emotional stability and financial security, most of all it means spiritual satisfaction. What a way to live!

Just before beginning the flamboyant faith chapter, the writer to the Hebrews said, "Now the just shall live by faith; but if anyone draws back, my soul has no pleasure in him" (Hebrews 10:38). This time as the Holy Spirit quotes Habakkuk, He seems to put the emphasis upon *faith*, for He follows it with a warning against apostasy, which is drawing back. The life that the "just" shall live is a life of *faith*.

Permit me to quote again from *Let Us Abide*:

"In the epistles of the New Testament ... we find at least sixteen areas of divine grace available to us through faith. For faith is listed as the source of, or channel for our: access to grace, healing, indwelling of Christ, justification, life, promise of the Spirit, propitiation, protection (shield and breastplate), righteousness, salvation, sanctification, standing, strength, steadfastness, understanding, and walk."

David found great security in living in the faith of Jehovah. He had no other source of provision, protection or guidance. Still, because of the unknown variables, living by faith can present its own set of insecurities. Someone has said, "A life of faith is like walking a precipice while surrounded by a miracle." There are risks to living by faith, but the rewards far outweigh the risks. The key to success is to always keep Christ Jesus as the object of our faith. He has never failed.

David spoke his faith

Anyone who has read the psalms of David knows that he spoke repeatedly of his trust in God. He declared, "Many are the afflictions of the righteous, but the LORD delivers him out of them all" (Psalm 34:19). He so lived in his faith that he dared to say: "The LORD redeems the soul of His servants, and none of those who trust in Him shall be condemned" (Psalm 34:22). He maintained a scriptural positive confession for the length of his life.

Faith and confession are inseparably linked in the Scriptures. Both Jesus and Paul established this incontestably.

> So Jesus answered and said to them, "Have faith in God. For assuredly, I say to you, whoever **says** to this mountain, 'Be removed and be cast into the sea,' and does not doubt in his heart, but believes that those things **he says** will come to pass, he will have whatever **he says**. Therefore I say to you, whatever things you ask **when you pray**, believe that you receive them, and you will have them" (Mark 11:22-24).

It seems impossible to read this without an awareness that the way we talk reveals and releases our faith in God. It is not what we speculate, but what we speak that produces action. Jesus was notable for the way He spoke His faith, for He spoke to the sea, and it immediately calmed; He spoke to a corpse, and life instantly returned to it; He spoke to a tree, and it withered. So forceful and producing were the words of Jesus that Simon Peter declared, "... You have the words of eternal life" (John 6:68). Christ always spoke with the authority of the Eternal God.

Paul not only practiced an open, positive confession, he proclaimed it to others in writing:

> But what does it say? "The word is near you, **even in your mouth** and in your heart" (that is, the word of faith which we preach): that if you confess **with your mouth** the Lord Jesus and believe in your heart that God has raised Him from the dead, you will be saved. For with the heart one believes to righteousness, and **with the mouth confession** is made to salvation (Romans 10:8-10).

The obvious key to conversion is the confession of the lordship of Jesus, not merely believing in our hearts. We must not only *see* Jesus as God's Christ; we must *say* what we see. We need to hear our mouths confess it, the demonic spirit world needs to be informed of our resignation, and God insists on hearing us confess His Son as our Lord and Savior.

Usually the word *confession* carries a negative connotation in religious circles. We are more apt to think of the confession of sin than the confession of righteousness. This confession is valid and vital to Christian experience. Once we confess our sin, the blood of Jesus cleanses us (see 1 John 1:9) and we no longer need to deal with that negative force. Christ dealt with it at Calvary. This leaves many Christians in a void or a vacuum as they retreat into their thought patterns, wondering what the future holds for them. They have not learned how to confess the Word of God as authoritative in their lives, nor have they fully grasped just who they are in Christ Jesus. Many continue to call themselves "only a sinner, saved by grace" long after the Scriptures call them saints in the making, sons in maturing, a Church under construction, and a bride in preparation. Their lack of understanding, or their unwillingness to confess what God's

Word says about them, keeps them from participating at a higher level with God.

David released his faith vocally

David experienced his share of troubled circumstances. He wrote: "Fear is on every side; while they take counsel together against me, they scheme to take away my life" (Psalm 31:13). Although he accurately described his situation, he refused to dwell on the negative. He vocally released his faith by declaring: "But as for me, I trust in You, O LORD; I say, 'You are my God.' My times are in Your hand ... " (Psalm 31:14-15) What a way to live in faith. David spoke his trust in God and released divine power for his deliverance.

It is fundamental that there is no release of faith without confession, for it is our confession that gives expression to the faith we have received from God. As long as we hold faith in our hearts, it remains an attitude. When we release it vocally, it becomes the basis for action.

Many writers call Christianity the great confession — an affirming of something sincerely believed. Christians testify to something they know from experience as well as their intellect. They witness to a truth they have embraced.

David's psalms abound with such confession. He sang, "But I have trusted in Your mercy; my heart shall rejoice in Your salvation. I will sing to the LORD, because He has dealt bountifully with me" (Psalm 13:5-6), and testified, "O my soul, you have said to the LORD, 'You are my Lord, my goodness is nothing apart from You' " (Psalm 16:2). He also exhorted others:

May the LORD answer you in the day of trouble;
may the name of the God of Jacob defend you;
may He send you help from the sanctuary, and
strengthen you out of Zion; may He remember all

*your offerings, and accept your burnt sacrifice.
Selah* (Psalm 20:1-3).

Obviously, David was accustomed to releasing his
faith vocally. He declared his faith to God, to his
friends, to his enemies and, often, to the problem.
David did not serve God silently. What was in his
heart came out his mouth. He comfortably declared
what he felt, but just as comfortably proclaimed what
he believed. If the two did not agree, he responded to
his faith and let his feelings get in line with that expression of faith.

For several years, there has been a fresh emphasis
on the truth of positively confessing our faith and
speaking to the seemingly unsurmountable problems.
The clear, concise command of Christ to speak to the
mountain always brings a vigorous, vibrant hope back
to the Church. This generation earnestly needs a
renewed hope, but we need a hope that goes beyond
positive feelings. We need more positive action based
on what God has said within our hearts. Some people
have received enough prophetic words over their lives
to last throughout eternity, but they have not changed
because those words are not mixed with faith. There is
neither confession nor action. Faith is not a pleasant
attitude. It is a concerted action.

David knew this. His faith was consistently active.
Whether it was in the use of weapons of war or in
teaching people to worship God, David made his faith
active, and his first action was vocal.

David did not create his faith

In every reemphasis of an abandoned truth, new
adherents tend to force the truth further than God's
revelation, thereby bringing the Church into error
through overemphasis. One wonders which is better:
error by underemphasis or error through overemphasis, for each is a deviation from the whole counsel
of God. Still, deviation through overemphasis seems to

frighten away honest seekers after truth far more than inaccuracy through underemphasis.

David would be horrified to see how far we have swung the pendulum in our generation. Instead of bringing people into God's glorious liberty, positive confession has left them bound in chains of frustration, introspection and guilt. Because it is the needy who turn to God, the faith message has had a great application to human suffering and God's provision of healing. Sick persons have been told to confess their healing and function as though they were completely whole. If faith flows through that confession, then the healing will become a reality; if God does not impart divine faith, no amount of confession will create it. Still the sick and infirm are instructed to confess their healing, ignore the symptoms, and keep both a positive attitude and a positive confession. If they fail in their confession, leaders often excommunicate them from the fellowship. Pastors have been dismissed from serving their congregations just because a member of the household died. It was declared to be an evidence of a lack of faith.

If our confession created faith, then that form of theology might hold true. But confession only *releases* faith, it does not create faith. The success of "he will have whatever he says" is dependent upon "have faith in God" (Mark 11:22-23). Until faith has been committed to us, it cannot be confessed by us. It is a dangerous oversimplification of truth to declare that *we* determine what we shall have by the words that we speak. This simplistic theology leads to half-truths, disappointments, frustrations and deep guilt.

Yet this idea of possessing creative power in our words is widely taught. We are told by way of radio, television, conferences and books that anything we desire is available to us if our concepts and confessions are correct. This distortion of the words of Jesus denies sickness to any "true believer," fails to come to grips with death, and chooses to ignore the dealings of God in the areas of privation, suffering, sickness or accident. All they view as negative they conveniently attribute to the devil, while all they define as good they ascribe to God.

It doesn't seem to matter to most of these disciples that this simplistic dualism won't stand the test of the whole Bible. Paul wrote to the saints at Corinth concerning their attitudes:

> *Even to the present hour we both hunger and thirst, and we are poorly clothed, and beaten, and homeless. And we labor, working with our own hands. Being reviled, we bless; being persecuted, we endure it* (1 Corinthians 4:11-12).

Paul would undoubtedly have been put out of the faith fellowship. Nor would Jesus, who lacked a place to lay His head, have been a good example to many faith exponents. If Jesus "learned obedience by the things which He suffered" (Hebrews 5:8) and was made "perfect through sufferings" (Hebrews 2:10), surely no amount of our confession can exempt us from similar dealings of God in our lives.

As Charles Farah, Jr. wrote in *From the Pinnacle of the Temple*:

> "Paul learned that although God wills health, we are not always healthy. He learned the secret not of total health but of total contentment (see Philippians 4:11). Paul clearly taught a Christian realism that admitted defeat when defeat had come, and hindrances when there had been hindrances."

This is consistent with David's attitude of faith. His trust in God was unwavering whether he was leading an army into battle or fleeing from Absalom during the insurrection. He knew both the blessing of God and the severe chastening of God, yet he consistently kept his faith rooted in the living God. Therefore, David could resolutely testify: "But I have trusted in Your mercy; my heart shall rejoice in Your salvation. I will sing to the LORD, because He has dealt bountifully with me" (Psalm 13:5-6). Just as earnestly, he could plead: "Bring my soul out of prison, that I may praise Your name; the righteous shall surround me, for You shall deal bountifully with me" (Psalm 142:7). His faith never swayed with his circumstances, for his faith was founded on the changelessness of Almighty God.

David channeled his faith

It seems that the extreme positive-confession teaching enjoins us to focus on our desires rather than on the higher purposes of God. We expect such self-centeredness in infants, but maturity causes an adjustment to the will of the Father (both in the natural and in the spiritual). David wrote: "I delight to do Your will, O my God ..." (Psalm 40:8) To confess what God wants for my life is one thing; to confess what I want for my life is quite another.

Joel Chandler Harris once said, "Watch out when you're getting all you want; fattening hogs ain't in luck." Still, any theology that puts creative power in the mouths of its adherents will be a popular theology, for it appeals to the American dream of affluence.

David did not believe that the divine message said that he was the captain of his ship or the controller of his destiny. He felt the true message was making God the sovereign Lord of his life. David recognized that there is great insecurity in being totally in charge of our destiny, for then one slip of the lip could bring sickness, accident or financial ruin. It was far more comfortable for him to accept that "the angel of the LORD encamps all around those who fear Him, and delivers them" (Psalm 34:7) than to have to combat the powers of hell, poverty, sickness and disaster with positive confession.

Although, in all honesty, we must admit that the modern Church has underplayed her authority in Christ, is it justifiable to overstate her authority? Can't we come back into balance as believers and return God to His creative throne? We need to become His dependent children, gladly confessing what He has said to us and done for us. If the eleventh chapter of Hebrews is, indeed, the model of how faith works, we must recognize that before it speaks of the working faith of Abel, Enoch, Noah or David, it declares: "By faith we understand that the worlds were framed by the word of God, so that the things which are seen were not made of things which are visible" (Hebrews 11:3). The first step in faith is dependence upon God. He is the Creator — we are not. We submit to Him; He does not bow to us. He speaks into existence; we can only say what He says.

Positive confession? Yes! David had it long ago. But not confession to create faith, for faith has its origins in God Himself. The purpose of positive confession is to release faith to the problem or circumstance by saying to the situation what God has said to us. This may give us God's power of attorney, but it doesn't make gods out of us. Our authority is totally delegated, our power is conferred, and our faith has been received. We produce none of it; we only proclaim it.

Any faith that cannot come to grips with reality is not a biblical faith. Daniel did not deny the reality of the lions or his precarious position with them in the den, but his faith preserved him in the midst of it. David never denied the actuality of Saul's pursuit or the Philistine aggression, but his active faith made him a victor over both enemies. Jesus never denied the reality of sickness, disease or death, but His divine faith overcame it beautifully. Faith that demands hypnotic denial of the existence of negative factors in our lives is more cultic than Christian.

David could never believe that faith was an exercise of mind over matter. He believed that faith is a divine impartation that really matters! Perhaps we need to ask ourselves whether faith changes our attestation or our attainment. Faith, as Jesus spoke of it, should change our circumstances, not merely our confession. It should also affect crisis situations, not merely produce Christian speech.

If David were alive today, he would plead for a return to the clear, concise, consecutive instruction of the whole Word of God as the only safe source of teaching on living faith that works. Perhaps if we will return to the pure, simple, divine faith of the Scriptures, we will have more results and less recrimination. Then we can move from false faith to true faith.

Chapter 14

David Worshiped
With a Fervent Faith

Faith's Passion

From its origin to the ocean, the Columbia River worships God. It is not merely that it seems to sing as it flows down the rapids or that it reflects the beauty of the heavens above in its wide-open stretches. It worships because it does what it is supposed to do, and it does it consistently. Everything in nature worships God by fulfilling the role God purposed for it when He created it. Bees worship when they cross-pollinate plants and make honey. Birds worship by eating insects and reproducing after their kind. Flowers worship when they burst forth into bloom according to the pattern chosen by the divine Creator. Surely, then, the rivers express their worship when they drain excess water from the land, flow to the ocean and give life to men, mammals, birds and fish.

David worshiped as a lifestyle

We human beings, having a much higher intellect, can vocalize our thanksgiving, sing our praise and perform a variety of rituals as acts of worship. Still, wouldn't our highest act of worship be to fulfill the purpose that God had in mind when He created us? David seemed to grasp this view, for he sensed that he was worshiping when he was doing what God told him to do. David worshiped while tending his father's sheep. He worshiped when singing before a demonized King Saul. He worshiped while he hid in caves and in wooded areas, waiting for God's timing to place him on the throne. David worshiped as a leader of men, and he worshiped on the battlefield while engaged in the bloody slaughter of an enemy. He worshiped when he brought the Ark to Jerusalem, and he worshiped when he was driven from Jerusalem. David believed that everything he did could be done as an act of worship before Almighty God.

While Psalm 150 does not have a title ascribing it to David, it has David's nature all the way through it. This is the way he lived:

Praise the LORD! Praise God in His sanctuary; praise Him in His mighty firmament! Praise Him for His mighty acts; praise Him according to His excellent greatness! Praise Him with the sound of the trumpet; praise Him with the lute and harp! Praise Him with the timbrel and dance; praise Him with stringed instruments and flutes! Praise Him with loud cymbals; praise Him with high sounding cymbals! Let everything that has breath praise the LORD. Praise the LORD! (Psalm 150)

No one in the Bible proved that worship is a lifestyle any better than David. The two times he spared King Saul's life were acts of worship onto the Lord. He would not touch God's anointed. David prayed as an act of worship. He not only saw his warfare as a worship service to God, but he built the Tabernacle of David and prepared for perpetual musical ministry to be offered unto Jehovah. He was a worshiper who prepared to bring others into worship with him.

After David had been crowned king, he reigned as an act of worship. He offered his people righteous judgment and faithful administration, for he knew that he ruled at God's command. David felt that he had "come to the kingdom for such a time as this" (see Esther 4:14), and every act of his administration became an expression of his worship.

David enjoyed the special feast days when he worshiped in harmony and fellowship with other covenant people, but he did not need this to be a worshiper. David never divorced worship from life. Three times a year he participated in these public worship sessions, but 365 days a year David worshiped Jehovah in the normal activities of the day. He had learned to practice the presence of the Lord and respond to it in service.

David's reign was an act of worship from the beginning to the end. He rejoiced in God's promise of a kingdom and responded in faith as God began preparing him to take the kingdom. When he accepted at Hebron the responsibilities of ruling over Judah, David worshiped. Three years later when Israel called him to reign over Judah as well, David again worshiped Jehovah who had chosen him.

Neither David's faith nor worship were put on. Most persons would loudly protest that they would never be deceitful concerning faith or worship. Still many continually try to grow faith by planting seeds. Some years ago, I was associated with a church that invited a guest minister whose ministry often took him behind the Iron Curtain. His financial need was apparent, so we took up an offering to help undergird his ministry. The following week a woman in that congregation told me that God had touched her and the heart of her husband to invest a sizable amount of money in this man's ministry. They agreed on a specific amount and sent it to Mr. X (a well-known television personality at the time). She assured me that the harvest of this seed would fully finance the guest minister's next trip to Europe.

Of course, it didn't. Faith cannot be grown, nor does giving money to one who has an obvious surplus meet the need of one who is lacking. This couple neither obeyed God nor functioned in divine faith. They played the well-known Christian game, "Let's Grow Faith," and left the responsibility of helping to meet this brother's financial plight up to the rest of us.

In Paul's list of things the Christian should "put on," faith is conspicuous by its absence. He challenges us to put on mercies, kindness, humility, meekness, longsuffering, forbearance, forgiveness, charity and peace (see Colossians 3:12-14), but he excluded faith from this list because faith can no more be put on — in the sense of being produced or grasped — and added to life than eternal life can be put on. Faith must be received and then lived. It is a life of faith, not an article of faith, of which the Bible speaks. Faith is not an addition to our lives; it is the vital energy of our lives.

Some have likened faith to the roots of a tree that supports the main trunk and limbs, while calling the leaves and fruit the grace of God. But Dr. Charles Price denies this allegory, insisting that faith is the life force that flows into the roots and then up throughout the entire structure of the tree. For faith does more than just stabilize the Christian's life; it gloriously animates it. David demonstrated this repeatedly.

Faith draws from the soil of the Word of God, converts it to a usable energy, and then transports it to the uttermost extremes of our lives. Fortunately, we need not understand it to experience it, for faith always works both in and through our lives to such an extent that we can be "full of faith" (Acts 6:8), "strong in faith" (Romans 4:20) and "steadfast in faith" (Colossians 2:5). We cannot reproduce that faith; we must receive it.

David made no attempt to produce faith. He simply received it from God and then released it back to God as an act of worship. Some of those acts didn't look very religious or worshipful, but they were filled with the faith God had imparted. David functioned the way God planned for him to function, with a high level of worship.

David worshiped with God's faith

Although there is a "natural faith," there is also a form of faith that is merely called the "faith *of* God." Jesus challenged His disciples to "have the faith of God" (Mark 11:22, marginal reading). Admittedly, most translators have chosen to say "faith in God," but in the Greek, "God" is the genitive case, which allows either translation with equal justification. The issue lies in whether God is the object of the faith or the subject of that faith (where it is possessive and represents God's own faith). Obviously, the context must decide the issue, and in the verses surrounding this text, Jesus had cursed the fruitless fig tree, which withered and died overnight. When the amazed disciples marveled at this miracle, Jesus said, "Have the faith of God," and then proceeded to explain to them how, with God's own faith operating through them, they could cast mountains into the sea with a verbal command (see Mark 11:20-24).

Paul seemed to grasp this concept, for he wrote: "I have been crucified with Christ; it is no longer I who live, but Christ lives in me; and the life which I now live in the flesh I live by faith in the Son of God, who loved me and gave Himself for me" (Galatians 2:20). If we substitute the word *Jehovah* for Christ, this could have been David's testimony. He lived his entire life in God's faith. David lived his worship; worship was a lifestyle to him. How it would thrill God if that were so in believers today!

Like David, Paul did not live, move, minister and function in his faith, but in the faith of the Son of God. Paul learned to lay hold of God's faith as the energy and force of his life. Everything that issued from his carnal nature had been crucified with Christ, and in exchange, he lived a quickened life that was sustained and energized by God's own faith. What a glorious exchange: Christ's life for ours, His faith for ours, His love for ours. David enjoyed such an exchange, and he used them all in his worship of Jehovah.

How great this level of God-like faith must be! Imagine having access to the unlimited, unwavering, inexhaustible faith of God that spoke the worlds into existence, formed man out of the dust of the earth, and continues to control everything He has created. "Have God's faith" must have been a command beyond the disciples' mental comprehension or volitional ability to respond.

Or was it so much a command as a commitment? When Christ says, "Have ... ," it is an offering of a gift, similar to our saying, "Have a mint," as we stretch forth our hand to make the candy available to the recipient. "Have the faith of God" is an offering of that limitless faith. Jesus had it, Paul had it, David had it, and we, too, may have it, for Jesus is "the author and finisher of our faith" (Hebrews 12:2). Jesus is the Author, Pioneer and Originator of our faith. Thus, this faith *of* God does not have its origin in the beliefs of man, but in the very nature of God Himself. Faith begins and ends in Him, so nothing we can do will manufacture it. Faith must be imparted by God.

How puny our weak human faith looks when we lay it alongside God's almighty faith. Sad as that comparison may be, consider how tragic it is when we label that impotent faith as divine faith. The difference in the faiths is not the label, but the source. What originates in God is divine faith, and what originates in man is human faith, no matter what the label reads.

David realized that the faith *of* God must come from God. He is its only source, and He has an eternal monopoly on its distribution. Divine faith cannot be synthesized or counterfeited. Neither can it be purchased or bargained for. Divine faith is never given as a reward, and its formula remains forever the secret of God. Man's participation in this faith is by the grace of God as He imparts it as a free gift. We cannot induce God to impart it by fasting and prayer; nor can any form of religious incantations bring it into the midst of a congregation of people. It is totally God's faith as to origin, transmission, conduct and control.

Mercifully, God imparted divine faith to David on many occasions. This is giant-killing faith. This is faith that pits a few hundred soldiers against an army that looks like the sand of the sea. This is faith that retakes Jerusalem from the Jebusites and makes it the capital of Israel. This is the unstoppable, inexhaustible and energetic faith *of* God that carries us into the realized presence of Jehovah and enables us to join with the angels and the spirits of just men made perfect in their worship around the throne of God. David experienced times of divine faith worship.

David's faith-filled worship was productive

We may have an abundance of faith in our lives without allowing it to affect the productivity of our lives or our worship. This is true because faith does not stand alone. Faith is supportive and assistive, but it is not complete. It must be directed to an object to be productive. Faith is not worship, but it can gloriously energize our worship. Faith can irrigate, but it does not propagate. Trust, the Old Testament word for faith, is no greater than the object in which the trust is vested. David realized this, for he wrote: "As for God, His way is perfect; the word of the LORD is proven; He is a shield to all who trust in Him" (Psalm 18:30). David did not see his trust as a shield because Jehovah was His protection. It was the combination of David's faith and Jehovah's response that was so productive.

Similarly, it is God's faith and our response in worship that makes such a powerful combination. David's worship was fervent because it was energized with fervent faith that came from God.

When, by God's sovereign grace, the faith of God begins to manifest itself through a believer, it does not become a resident gift, nor is that individual given the liberty to use the faith according to his or her will. God, who imparts this faith, also directs its operation. We are the channels for faith's flow, not its controllers. The same limitation that makes it impossible for a person to produce a divine force makes it dangerous for that human to have the control of a divine force. God imparts His faith for a specific purpose then withdraws it from the grasp of persons. Leaving it resident with people would be as dangerous as allowing a two-year-old to have a loaded pistol among his playthings.

God's faith, His impartation of faith, and His control of that imparted faith are amazingly productive. God's faith parted the Red Sea, opened the earth to swallow Korah, and rained daily manna upon Israel. God's faith cleansed the lepers, opened blind eyes, and raised the dead. This divine faith can do anything and everything that God decrees, for, as Dr. Charles Price said, *"You can't have faith without results any more than you can have motion without movement."*[1] Since this is God's faith, it will have God's results, and they are always tremendous in man's opinion. My! How it produces worship of the highest nature!

---

1.   *The Real Faith*, Dr. Charles Price, p. 74.

When David found himself in a situation beyond his faith level, he spent time in God's presence and received new faith to meet the challenge. When everything else failed to meet his needs, David learned to lift his eyes above the needs to the Need-Meeter. Today's Christians need to follow David's lead. We need to shift our gaze from faith itself to the God of that faith, for we need the Energizer far more than we need His energy. The true issue isn't our relationship to things, needs, believing, confession or even our faith. The real issue is our relationship to God Himself. The closer and warmer that relationship becomes, the greater the availability of God's faith will be.

David discovered that he could not function without faith. Nor could he successfully produce divine faith. Thus, he either had to find God to receive His faith or he had to fake it. David knew that faking it could be deadly. We too can either accept God's divine energy or we can act as though we have it. We can live in faith or we can pretend we have faith. If we choose the latter, we forfeit the power in our lives of productive worship.

David worshiped with a fervent faith

Since David lived ardently, it is to be expected that he would worship fervently. Everything he did was done with zest and zeal. He lived life to the fullest. Whatever his hands found to do, he did with all his might. When it came time for worshiping his God, King David brought that same enthusiasm with him. Unlike some modern men who enjoy sports excitedly on Saturday but worship God in boredom on Sunday, David worshiped Jehovah the way he lived — fervently.

David's fervent faith was practical because faith always produces. It does not come to excite, but to execute something. Things happens when we release faith. Faith saves, faith heals, faith obeys and faith cleanses. Faith reaches into the unseen world and brings visible evidence into the seen world. Faith is active, never passive.

When Jesus exercised faith, the fig tree dried up from its roots, bread and fish were multiplied to feed vast multitudes, blind eyes were opened, demons were cast out, and even the dead were raised. His faith was potent and productive because it was rooted in God and released to men. It calmed the storm, walked on the water, turned water into wine, and rode an untrained donkey in a parade of shouting people.

Similar things can be said of David's faith. When it functioned, he overcame the demonic spirits that troubled King Saul. His fervent faith also conquered new territory and subdued enemies. This faith united a nation, transforming tribalism into nationalism for Israel. His fervent faith released others to enter ministry, and this same faith built a temple. This fervent faith of David burned through every act of worship, putting a flame to the incense. Worship that lacks luster is impotent, emotionless and faithless. Faith-filled worship works to conquer new territory for God. It subdues the strongholds satan has in our minds and unites the body of Christ in the unity of the Church. When we worship in the level of faith David used in his worship, we, too, will build a temple onto the Lord, for we are the temple of the living God.

David was convinced that we must be participants, not spectators, in worship. He sacrificed, sang and danced before the Lord. He prayed, both in private and in public. When it was time for worship, David willingly laid aside his kingly robes and girded himself with the linen ephod of a priest. He did not want honor, for he had come to give glory and honor onto the Lord.

David was a multi-faceted man. He fascinates me. This is my third book on the life of David, and I still don't feel I have come even close to exhausting the riches his life exposes for the believer. It is obvious that he was a man of real faith who released that faith to meet a great variety of needs and problems. David's favorite release of faith, however, was in worship. When he worshiped, he worshiped fervently and passionately. Never did he worship half-heartedly or absent-mindedly. For as long as he lived, David worshiped God in every aspect of his life and with his whole heart. Because his spirit was inflamed with love for Jehovah, worship set his whole being on fire.

THINGS WE ADORE by *Judson Cornwall*. This vital message looks at the beginnings of idolatry, searching out the roots deep in the ground of the Old Testament, and lays that idolatry alongside that of the modern Church. From doctrines of demons to the idols of men in high places, the things we adore have become the greatest threat to the Church's purity and genuine relationship with her Lord. This book will challenge you to allow the Holy Spirit to search your heart, letting His light reveal the idols that keep you from true fulfillment. TPB-224p. ISBN 1-56043-048-6 Retail $8.99

DAVID WORSHIPED A LIVING GOD by *Judson Cornwall*. This is Judson's newest book on praise and worship, destined to become a classic as it describes in beautiful detail the names of God and what they mean to the worshiping saint. TPB-182p. ISBN 0-938612-38-7 Retail $8.99

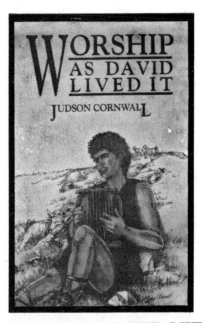

WORSHIP AS DAVID LIVED IT by *Judson Cornwall*. This is part two of a trilogy about David's heart and life as a worshiper. This book will show you the intimacy and the necessity of God's nearness as it is discovered in a life of worship. TPB-196p. ISBN 1-56043-700-6 Retail $8.99

LEADERS: EAT WHAT YOU SERVE by *Judson Cornwall*. Burned out. Dropped out. Forced out. These dreadful terms have become too commonly used when describing those who carry the mantle of servanthood in the church. Yet there are ways of dealing with these situations that are most often found in our own sermon notebooks. Leaders must learn to EAT WHAT YOU SERVE. The same relationship with Jesus that we encourage others with is the same relationship that changes and strengthens the leader's life as well. TPB-238p. ISBN 0-914903-59-4 Retail $7.99

SECRETS OF THE MOST HOLY PLACE by *Don Nori.* Here is a prophetic parable you will read again and again. The winds of God are blowing. They are drawing you to His Life within the Veil of the Most Holy Place. There you begin to see as you are seen, know as you are known and experience a depth of relationship that your heart has been yearning for. Secrets long hidden to the casual and passive believer are wonderfully opened to those who diligently seek Him. This is not a teaching book or a theological exegesis. It is a living and dynamic experience with God! TPB-182p. ISBN 1-56043-076-1 Retail $8.99